Cat Women

female writers on their
feline friends

edited by
Megan McMorris

SEAL PRESS

Published by
Seal Press
An Imprint of Avalon Publishing Group, Incorporated
1400 65th Street, Suite 250
Emeryville, CA 94608

ISBN-13: 978-1-58005-203-0
ISBN-10: 1-58005-203-7

Library of Congress Cataloging-in-Publication Data

Cat women : female writers on their feline friends / edited by Megan McMorris.
p. cm.
ISBN-13: 978-1-58005-203-0
ISBN-10: 1-58005-203-7
1. Cats—Anecdotes. 2. Women cat owners—Anecdotes. 3. Human-animal relationships—Anecdotes. I. McMorris, Megan.

SF445.5.C392 2007
636.8'0887—dc22

2006038572

Cover and interior design by Domini Dragoone
Printed in the United States of America by Malloy
Distributed by Publishers Group West

To Mitzi (1976-1991),
Mattie (1993-2001),
Lucy (2000-2004), and
Lily (2000-)

Contents

Note from the Editor:

We're Cat Ladies, So Sue Us

Megan McMorris

A funny thing happened on my way to putting together this book. When I started spreading the word to all the female-writers-with-cats I knew (or knew of), a common theme emerged: Women were a little sheepish—*apologetic*, even—about owning a cat. "Well, I own a cat, but I'm really a dog person," they'd say. Or, "I have three cats, but it's not like I'm a crazy cat lady or anything!" Any acknowledgment of owning a cat came with the B word afterward: *but* (as in, "Sure I have a cat, *but* . . . ").

I have to admit that even I fell into this habit. When friends would ask what I'd been working on lately, I'd kinda breeze through a description of this book, and quickly add, "But it's going to be cool, not cheesy!" Funny, somehow I never felt compelled to add these PSs when I described the dog version of this book, which I edited and which came out last year (*Woman's Best Friend: Women Writers on the Dogs in Their Lives*, if you must know).

Even though some of the authors were hesitant to admit their companion animal of choice, their love for the little furballs became clear once I started asking for pictures of the cats to illustrate the essays. "Do you prefer kitten or adult?" asked one writer. Others just went ahead and sent in mini cat-photo scrapbooks. One thing was certain: We all get a little shutter-happy when there's a feline around (the record submission was nine photos of one cat, in various poses and stages of life, warming the lap of each family member). Let's just say that if we had decided to turn this into a photo book, I'd have had plenty of material to work with.

So what's the deal? If we love our cats so much (and you know we do), why are these intelligent, successful women ashamed to admit they have cats? It's something that I vowed to get to the bottom of, and I encouraged writers to make it their theme. The results: Lisa L. Goldstein muses about whether she's crossed the crazy-cat-lady line in "Call Me Crazy . . . My Life as a Cat Lady," while Jenna Schnuer examines how (and why) she emphasizes the macho side of her cat in her witty tale "Admitting Maynard." Finally, Clea Simon takes an interesting look at what started this whole female/cat link in the first place in "The

Feline-Female Connection," and considers why society is still so mystified—threatened, even—by our famous pairing.

As for myself, I've been a front-seat fan of cats ever since I can remember, and I don't apologize for it. I admire their grace, their independence, and the aloof-yet-loving balance that's second nature to felines (not to mention their handy ability to clean themselves!). For nearly thirty years, I've had a little furry presence sharing my living space. First was my childhood cat in Ohio, a brown tabby named Mitzi, who was so aloof that our family would celebrate if she deigned to grace one of our laps with her warm presence. She lived until I was twenty-one, and was followed by a sleek, glamorous NYC tuxedo cat, Mattie, who would dazzle my guests with her fetching ability (she had a special affinity for straws). A decade and a cross-country move later, brown tabby Lily and black cat Lucy (RIP) entered my life, and shared an old, spooky barn where I lived in Hood River, Oregon. They liked to wrestle with each other before retiring to their little beds on either side of the fireplace.

No matter what their stripe or color, or what living arrangement I've had, cats have ushered me through all stages of my life. I *get* them.

That's why it was especially fun to put together this collection, keeping in mind what we *all* love about cats. From their desire to Get Outside or Bust (and then either panic and run up a tree or just stand there, not really knowing what to do) to the sophisticated, royal way that they curl their tails around their bodies and look at you with slit eyes, or sit in the middle of the room with their backs to you when they're miffed, cats are fascinating and funny little creatures. And let's face it, there's nothing like a warm, furry body purring and kneading on your lap.

With cats, it's all about the subtleties in personality, small differences only cat people understand—like the tiny snoring sounds coming from underneath my desk as I type this (and when I look underneath to find the source of the noise, there she is on her bed, curled up with her paw over her eyes), or the way she looks annoyed at me after I give her a big, sloppy kiss on her tummy, before she starts maniacally cleaning my kiss off.

Rather than collecting me-and-my-cat-walking-paw-in-hand-into-the-sunset stories, I wanted this book to examine all aspects of felines and how they affect our lives. The tales range from witty (Lynne Truss laments a lack of Valentines from the cats in "Making the Cat Laugh: One Woman's Journal of Single Life on the Margins") to tear-provoking (Susan Schulz Wuornos offers up a tribute to Murphy in "An Ode to the Murph Dawg") to downright wacky (Dimity McDowell visits a local cat show and leaves with lessons learned the hard way in "Hang with Scrappy T [and Other Rules of the Cat-Show Road]").

There's one thing I hope this book is not, of course: apologetic. I wanted this book to be a tribute to the furry friends in our lives, without a hint of the B word.

Thanks for reading.

Megan Mc Morris

March 2007

The Cat That Got Away

Sophia Dembling

It was December 22, 1986, when Aretha left me. I admit we hadn't been getting along. I had been spending a lot of time away from home—working late, staying out nights, taking vacations. She was neglected and peeved. I can't say that I blame her. When she left me, I was packing to go to my parents' for Christmas.

I saw her slip out the door as I opened it for friends. I didn't chase her. I figured she'd come home by dinnertime.

She wasn't an easy cat to live with. She was big and demanding, and her long, black fur detached itself with lavish abandon. She had subtle and devious methods of getting her way, like casually draping her sweeping tail across my nose to get me up in the morning. She lived to eat, and I had spoiled her rotten with table scraps. Most men detested her.

But she was affectionate when she felt like it, and was a sympathetic listener. I knew she was rude, but it had been she and I for so long—nearly ten years—that I assumed it would be she and I forever. Roommates. Sisters. Pals.

But she didn't return that day. I was worried, but Aretha had street smarts and I had airline tickets. I left town as planned,

Aretha

with reassurances from my neighbor, who was cat-sitting. I checked in daily, but Aretha didn't return. Not while I was gone, or after I came home. My neighbor said she'd spotted her hanging out with some other neighborhood cats in the back yard. Impossible, I said. Aretha attacked anything with fur or feathers. She'd once sent a full-grown Dalmatian hightailing it home. She wouldn't socialize with strays.

A couple of days later, I saw her. She was sitting in my neighbor's back yard. She looked at me when I called her name. When I approached, she turned and ran.

She wasn't lost. She wasn't hurt. She wasn't stolen.

She had left me.

I noticed a bunch of other cats hanging around. There was a gray male with a red collar, a raggedy orange and white female who seemed to be eternally in heat, a mangy little tabby male, and a long-haired tortoiseshell who lived at the piano tuner's house across the street. Aretha tolerated the gray one, ignored the rest.

I tried wooing her back with bowls of Purina left on the back step. Everyone except Aretha made an appearance. Each would have a furtive snack, then skulk away, with backward, embarrassed looks at me. Even after I gave up this endeavor, one cat or another would slither up to the door every time I opened it—just to make sure I didn't have some tasty treats for them.

I shouldn't have kept Aretha indoors so much. She was athletic. My apartment—which was in a fourplex—was just three rooms, and I let her out into the yard only when I was around to keep an eye on her.

Now I wanted to talk things over with her, tell her I'd made a mistake, that things would be different. But things already were different. I couldn't tell her anything anymore.

A month passed. The other cats set up a clubhouse in the backyard shed. Aretha made an appearance every couple of days. If I spotted her, she'd look me in the eye and run away.

The other cats watched me. I often spotted ears and eyes up against the screen door. Sometimes—if the opportunity arose—one of them would just stroll casually into the house. I'm not sure if they were planning the perfect punishment for cat abuse or considering applying for Aretha's old position.

Aretha looked perfectly content. I guess she found herself a new home, the way she had found me on a New York street. She had just walked up to me and demanded attention. It worked.

If you love something, let it go, et cetera. There is solace in that, I suppose. I thought she was my cat. I was mistaken.

Months passed. The last time I saw Aretha, she was sitting on my neighbor's roof. I approached her, cooed at her, asked her to come home. She jumped off the roof and landed in a bouncy heap. One quick scramble and she was on her feet, poised at the top of a fence. She turned to give me an "I recognize the face but can't place the name" look before she tore out of sight.

That was twenty years ago.

The other cats settled in the shed. A Siamese half-breed and a big, silver tabby joined the club. The gray cat, too, though he still wore a red collar. I suppose somebody thought this meant he was owned.

Eventually I moved away. Did Aretha notice? I'll never know. But as far as I'm concerned, she's still out there, prowling the streets. (No, don't tell me otherwise. I find comfort in believing she's immortal.)

Admitting Maynard
Jenna Schnuer

The gift of a needlepoint cat pillow nearly did me
in. Maynard, the kitten I had taken up with, was
threatening to upend my reputation. Sure, I was single, but I
wasn't *single with cat*, a phrase that should mean nothing but is
layered with spinster jokes and tinged with pathetic.

If anything, I was a dog person who just happened to own a
cat. I lived in a studio apartment on the fourth floor of a walk-up.
It wasn't just no-dogs-allowed territory, it was a (lack of) space
guaranteed to make a canine miserable. I didn't really want a cat
but I did want a pet, and, with fourth grade long over, hamsters
and guinea pigs didn't seem all that rewarding anymore. And
fish just don't do it for me. So, when friends who already owned
a cat—and couldn't take on another—found a kitten in a parking

17

lot, I decided to take him in. On his chin he sported a black goatee that reminded my friends of Maynard G. Krebs, Bob Denver's character on the 1960s TV show *The Many Loves of Dobie Gillis*. No other names were considered. It was perfect. The name was far from precious. It was more character than cat.

But shortly after, my mom, my hip mom, the woman who

Maynard

had seen me turn from a tomboy of a girl into a no-frills T-shirt and jeans kind of woman, the one who knew I favored graphics that tended toward harder-edged themes (think skulls), gave me the needlepoint cat pillow. My perception of the way other people viewed me splintered into thin cracks. If just one freakishly hyper, one-and-a-half-pound cat could change my mom's take on my personality, I was doomed.

While so many people claim to be the last group in America you're allowed to make fun of, it's doubtful that single cat owners would ever be taken seriously for protesting. Single cat owner that I am, I'm just as guilty of thinking that owning a cat is a negative personality trait. *Single cat owner.* It's just a step away from *Great Expectations*'s Miss Havisham and her moldy wedding cake. Cat ownership doesn't say *I'm an independent woman,* it says *Comfort me now—and constantly.* The only dog owners who automatically dwell in this land of preciousness are those who dress their teacup Malte-poos in mini sweat suits.

Thirteen years into cohabitation with Maynard (and Maynard alone), my desire to be labeled *single cat owner* hasn't grown any. Maynard definitely has. He's a twenty-pound bruiser with an attitude to match (and, at times, a bit of a split personality). He's exactly the cat I deserve.

There is no (or very little) preciousness here. At least, there's not much I'll admit to publicly. Instead, during conversations about cats with people I don't know well (and the damned creatures have a way of coming up in conversation more often than not), I resort to my verbal tic—*I'm a dog person but I own a cat*—and share tales of Maynard misbehavior.

I let them in on the dangers of brushing Maynard. After a few minutes of calm, he tenses into hunting stance. If I move away too slowly, my collection of bite marks gets a plus one. I risk my audience thinking I'm a bad pet owner and tell them how it's been years since I willingly cut his nails. Instead, I leave his nail care to his constant scratching of my rug (he uses the scratching post as a place to nap) or, once Maynard is sedated for an exam (it takes two shots to manage him), to the vet. I make daily life seem like one of my travel adventures, describing how I have to remain vigilant when I'm barefoot, scanning the room for the beast. If I let down my guard, he's liable to clamp his teeth down on my ankle, letting go only to bite my wrist when I try to pull him off. The stories aren't lies. I have the scars to prove it.

Some friends protest that, in conversation, I all too often paint Maynard as the brute, that I don't give enough attention to his sweeter side. I'm finally willing to admit this is true. It *is* unfair. But cat talk isn't really all that interesting to me. And I'm already fighting against a world of thoughts (both real and imagined) about single women in their late thirties. I don't need another undeserved black mark on my personality. I don't want people to concentrate on my labels; I want them to concentrate on my life.

There's just one little problem: When Maynard falls asleep, he puts his paw over his eyes to block out the light. And it's so freakin' cute that I have to mention it. And just like that, I'm *single with cat*—although, in all fairness, I did throw out the pillow.

Hang with Scrappy T
(and Other Rules of the Cat-Show Road)

Dimity McDowell

My childhood cat, Tinkerbell, had U-shaped ears. Valleys where there should have been mountains. One frigid Minnesota night, when I called her inside for the tenth time, she still wouldn't come—she was probably sick of me quarantining her under my covers—so I gave up. She was meowing at the door at 5:00 the next morning. By 5:00 PM, the tips of her ears had hardened to scabs, and twenty-four hours later, victims of frostbite, they fell off.

A few beers with the right crowd and, okay, Tink's special-needs ears are good for some laughs. The wrong crowd with which to share such a tale? The cat lovers—cat fanciers, as they call themselves—who are exhibiting their felines at the twenty-ninth annual Rocky Mountain Cat Fanciers' Association cat show, an event I read about in the local paper and decide to check out. Because my husband is allergic, I haven't held a cat in years and am craving some feline loving.

As soon as I walk into the City Auditorium in downtown Colorado Springs, I vow to keep my trap shut about Tinkerbell. The 169 pedigreed felines competing in the show not only have intact ears, they are also impeccably groomed. What's more, they don't go outside, don't eat Meow Mix, and have probably never tasted a mouse in any of their nine lives.

While there are certain predictable things you can expect at a cat show—wry, feline-themed sweatshirts declaring, WE GOT RID OF THE KIDS. THE CAT WAS ALLERGIC, for one—there is much more you wouldn't expect. So on the off chance you find yourself surrounded by cat fanciers in the heat of competition, here are five rules you should know.

Rule number one: These cats are *not* like your cat.

First of all, show cats cost money. Big bucks. At least a couple hundred, or, if the cat is a male whose dangly bits are still dangling, at least a grand. The $50 adoption fee you coughed up for a Humane Society variety would only cover a year's supply of jarred Gerber turkey baby food, the feline meal of choice at the show. The liver-colored food is typically served on a spoon, and if the cat has copious amounts of hair, it is probably wearing a lacy bib to keep its coat pristine.

Secondly, does your cat have a name like Thunderpoz Carrie of Katcus Koons? To be sure, these complicated names illustrate the cat's legacy (something that, I would venture to guess, most household pets don't have much of, either). The first word(s)—Thunderpoz—alludes to the cat's breeder, and the final words—Katcus Koons—indicate which cattery the feline came from. So Thunderpoz Carrie of Katcus Koons is probably just called Carrie at home, but her heritage still hangs in the air, unspoken. After all, even though you knew Jackie O as Jackie O, her full name was actually Jacqueline Lee Bouvier Kennedy Onassis.

The owners of these cats can quickly recite the parental lineage of each cat. For instance, Karmacatz Slumber Party was a result of Dillitante Napoleon of Karmacatz and Northshore Party Girl of Karmacatz getting frisky one afternoon. Even though her Party Girl moniker makes her seem like she'd always wear miniskirts in bars, the cat had some serious show credentials—most notably, regional winner—so be assured that their mating was the feline equivalent of an arranged marriage. In other words, Slumber Party's beginnings were far more calibrated than the crazy nights in alleys that produce generic

Fluffys and Spikes. There are cats, and then there are show cats. Please don't compare the two.

Rule number two: Keep your hands to yourself.

At the show, the competitors spend the majority of their time resting inside tiny tents of plastic and mesh that zip shut. Called security shelters by the fanciers, they're filled with everything from practical litter boxes to luxurious sheepskin-covered hammocks. They let air in, but keep hands out. If fanciers haven't sprung for shelters, their charges will be housed in show-provided cages, which they drape with towels or blankets to, again, discourage human contact. (By the way, they also decorate the cages with everything from feather boas to rhinestone crowns for the cage-decorating contest.)

If the signs on the cages, which range from simple, polite messages (PLEASE DON'T DISTURB) to the downright vitriolic (OWNER PSYCHOTIC: DON'T TOUCH THE DAMN CAT!), don't stop you from reaching out for the cute pink nose of Six Guns Shasta of Walkingstick, the owners will. Most owners spend the majority of the show perched in front of the shelter, either spoon-feeding their cats or entertaining them with a fancier's must-have accessory: a plastic stick with feathers on the end (a.k.a. a teaser). The owners do talk quietly among themselves, but they've usually got their backs to the crowds roaming the aisles. The effect makes you think twice about petting Shasta, or even twitching a teaser in front of her. At least, it should.

I, of course, learn this the hard way. My first morning at the show, Jack, a gentle sixty-something man, immediately befriends me, for reasons still unclear to me. I am grateful for his openness and willingness to talk about his Oriental shorthairs: Abyjack Max, Abyjack Tina, and Abyjack Kira. According to the Cat Fanciers' Association (CFA) breed standard, show-quality Orientals should have almond-shaped eyes, large, flared ears, and svelte, tubular bodies. To illustrate the last point, Jack makes both hands into L shapes with his thumbs and index fingers, puts one under Max's armpits and one under his hips, and stretches him out like a sausage. Max looks uncomfortable at best, so I reach out to pet his forehead. "Don't touch," Jack says rather forcefully. I apologize, withdraw my hands, and put them in my pockets, where they stay for most of the show.

Why the hands-off policy? Because the owners don't want you to dirty their cats' dainty paws. Every cat here has not only just had a bath, but also had its nails clipped, ears and bottom cleaned, and eyebrows trimmed. ("It makes their eyes look bigger," someone enlightens me.) Some cats, like the athletic, short-haired ocicats, are wash-and-wear types: a quick bath and they're good to go. Others, like the shedding nightmare Maine coons, require an hour plus to lather and rinse a degreasing agent, a color-emphasizing shampoo, and three other separate products into their long coats. For last minute touch-ups, many long-haired breeds have a grooming station, with essential products like Foo Foo grooming powder, next to their cages. A spectator touching fur during the show would be akin to putting a baseball hat on a perfectly coiffed bride right before she walked down the aisle.

But the main issue is disease. Communicable diseases can be passed from one cat to another, via an ambitious snotty-nosed kid who can't keep his paws to himself. Fair enough: Given the devotion, both economical and emotional, the owners have for their cats, it's understandable that they don't want just anyone touching their prized possessions. (Even though it doesn't exactly create a hospitable environment for us ignorant nonfanciers in the crowd!)

Rule number three: Don't expect the cats to walk around a ring.

These are cats who prefer to be carried, don't heed commands, and don't do tricks. Instead, they do a lot of sitting around during the judging. When the cat's number is called to one of four rings (each with its own judge), the owner, after brushing its fur one last time, deposits it in one of the twelve cages in the ring—ordered male/female/male/female to avoid cat fights—closes the door, and often twitches a teaser in front of the cat, just to make sure it's at its perkiest. The judge then pulls each cat out individually, stands the animal on a foot-high judging platform, strokes its fur, looks into its eyes, inspects the ears and tail, possibly bats a feather in front of it to get a reaction, then puts it back into the cage.

The competition isn't terribly interesting to watch, unless you happen to know that, according to the CFA, the head of a Bombay should be pleasingly rounded with no sharp angles; that the Egyptian mau's feet should be dainty and slightly oval; or that the Turkish Angora should have eyes with deep, rich tones. During a final round, when the top ten cats of a certain division are evaluated a second time, a judge does explain what she likes about a certain feline. Still, unless you're fluent with terms like "flared ear set," "deep nose break," and "squared-off muzzle," don't count on understanding why Purnpines Baby Doe beat Pendragon Ruby Dude.

After every cat has left its cage, the stewards—young kids earning $20 a day—spray the cages with disinfectant and dry them so they're clean for their next occupants. While they get the job done, they lack the alacrity of, say, a Wimbledon ball boy; in fact, Marco, a nine-year-old, cracks his Harry Potter novel less than one hour into the second day. I ask him if he gets bored, and he just smiles. Definitely not the makings for must-see television, even on Animal Planet.

Rule number four: Don't even *try* to figure out who won the thing.

After two days of asking questions about how cat shows are scored, I realize it's easier to launch a space shuttle than it is to figure out the system. I do, however, grasp that there are three main divisions: kittens, championship cats, and premier cats, which have been "altered" and won't be on any more family trees. The cats are also divided by sex, hair length, breed, and color. Please note: Despite what your eye may tell you, there are no brown, tan, or black cats here. Ocicats, for instance, are available in tawny (blackish), cinnamon (reddish), blue (diluted tawny), fawn (diluted cinnamon), and a couple other color-related adjectives commonly found in the J. Crew catalog.

The cats are judged in an endless variety of combinations—champions versus champions, tawnies versus tawnies, and so on—which nets a phalanx of metal ribbons that the judge places on the cages as quickly and thoughtlessly as a secretary can type. Each ribbon color represents some kind of win, but they're not worth much, cat-fancy-wise, kind of like participation ribbons in a grade-school soccer league. There is no applause when the metal ribbons are hung. In fact, they're reused throughout the day, and the stewards sometimes get a stern look if they forget to remove them during the sanitation process.

The finals, however, are what really count, both in recognition and competition. The best cats earn silky rosettes that rank them from first to tenth in a certain division, and these are proudly displayed on the security shelters. They also earn a certain number of points, based on their place and on how many cats they've beaten to secure their rosette. (This system is so complicated that more than one owner pulls out a laminated scoring card to try to explain it to me.) The best cats here will eventually become grand champions, which requires two hundred points and marks a step on the way to becoming a regional or national champion, both of which call for point totals in the thousands. Not that every cat necessarily will go for a more illustrious title, though: When I ask random owners if a young grand champion like Furensics Gunshot Residue will take it to the next level, they cite cost and politically influenced judges as hurdles too high to jump.

I can see their point: The system feels random. The rankings from each of the eight judges aren't combined, so you can't decisively say, "Playwickey Fudge Pop is absolutely the best cat at the show." And really, it seems that if you have a lot of disposable income with which to acquire a high-quality cat and then travel, you can buy yourself a regional or national champion ranking. Unlike winning a horse race, which requires athleticism from both the jockey and the horse, or a dog show, during which a canine has to respond to commands quickly, being awarded a rosette at a cat show seems to rely mostly on good feline genes and how well the owner can wield eyelash clippers.

Rule number five: Hang with Scrappy T and the other HHPs.

While my whole point in going to the cat show is to get familiar with the pedigreed world, I can't help but be drawn to the cats in the household pet (HHP) division. The HHPs are either Heinz 57 varieties or purebreds who fall pitifully short of CFA standards. There are only eleven of them here, so it's not hard to get on a first-name basis with them, especially because they have simple names like Cinderelli or Mr. Dinkers. For the most part, the owners are beginner fanciers. One family, here to show Abigail, didn't even wash her, a serious, serious cat-fancy sin. "She hates being bathed," the mom whispers to me. "There was no way we were doing that."

Scrappy T, a one-year-old off-the-street type with snow

white fur and grey stripes on his back, is instantly my favorite. He's got personality: In the ring, he pokes a paw through the cage to bat at the judge walking by, and back in his shelter, he lounges aloofly, on a pillow whose deep red seems more suited for a brothel than a cat show. His owner is an approachable woman named Molly who wears paw-print earrings and a shirt that

Scrappy T

reads, IF YOU WANT A FRIEND, GET A DOG. Every time Scrappy is brought out to the judging pedestal, she bellows in her Texas accent, oblivious to the hushed nature of the show, "Scrappy T! Scrappy T!" as if her cheering will lead him to victory. Molly is one of the few owners who explains things in ways I comprehend. I ask her what the extra fat around a particularly portly HHP is called. "Oh, that hunka hunka burning love?" she replies. "My vet calls it zoo gut."

Not only is the HHP crowd refreshingly relaxed, the judging for them is openly subjective (one judge explains, "Sometimes I like a cat, sometimes I don't") and straightforward (there are no points or titles on the line). After inspecting each of the eleven HHPs, the judge awards the top ten rosettes. To prevent hurt feelings—I hear again and again that today's HHP owners are tomorrow's true cat fanciers—the eleventh-place cat gets a catnip-filled mouse or other toy.

After Scrappy T nets his second first-place rosette, I feel buoyant and oddly attached to Scrappy and Molly. I even consider telling her about Tinkerbell and her ears in order to strengthen our bond. As she gathers Scrappy to take him back to his pad, though, I ultimately decide against it. After all, even the HHPs have standards.

Making the Cat Laugh:
One Woman's Journal of
Single Life on the Margins

Lynne Truss

No Valentines from the cats again. Sometimes I wonder whether they are working as hard at this relationship as I am. Few other pets, I imagine, were lucky enough to find their Valentine's Day breakfasts laid out on heart-shaped trays, with the words "From Guess Who" artfully arranged in Kitbits around the edge. But what do I get in return? Not even a single rose. Not even a "Charming thought, dear. Must rush." Just the usual unceremonious leap through the cat flap, the usual glimpse of the flourished furry backside, with its "Eat my shorts" connotation. Wearily I sweep up the Kitbits with a dustpan and brush and try to remember whether King Lear was talking about pets when he coined the phrase about the serpent's tooth.

Of course, the world would be a distinctly different place

if cats suddenly comprehended the concept of give-and-take—if every time you struggled home with a hundredweight of cat food and said accusingly, "This is all for you, you know," the kitties accordingly hung their heads and felt embarrassed. Imagine the scene on the garden wall:

"Honestly, guys, I'd love to come out. But the old lady gave me Sheba this morning, and I kind of feel obliged to stay home."

"She gave you *Sheba?*"

"Yeah. But don't go on about it. I feel bad enough that I can never remember to wipe my feet when I come in from the garden. When I think of how much she does for me . . . " *(breaks down in sobs).*

Instead, one takes one's thanks in other ways. For example, take the Valentine's present I bought them: a new catnip toy, shaped like a stick of dynamite. This has gone down gratifyingly well, even though the joke misfired slightly. You see, I had fancied the idea of a cat streaking through doorways with a stick of dynamite between its jaws, looking as though it had heroically dived into a threatened mine shaft and recovered the explosive just in time to save countless lives. In this *Lassie Come Home* fantasy, however, I was disappointed. Instead, cat number one reacted to the dynamite by drooling an alarming quantity of gooey stuff all over it (as though producing ectoplasm), then hugging it to his chest and trying to kick it to death with his back paws.

Yet all is not lost. If the cat chooses to reject the heroic image, I can still make the best of it. With a few subtle adjustments to my original plan, I can now play a highly amusing game with the other cat that involves shouting, "Quick! Take cover! Buster's got a stick of dynamite, and we'll all be blown sky-high!" And I dive behind the sofa.

I suppose all of this gratitude stuff has been brought to mind because I recently purchased a very expensive cat accessory, which has somehow failed to elicit huzzahs of appreciation. In fact, it has been completely cold-shouldered. Called a "cat's cradle," it is a special fleece-covered cat hammock that hooks onto a radiator. The cat is suspended in a cocoon of warmth. A brilliant invention, you might think. Any rational cat would jump straight into it. Too stupid to appreciate the full glory of my gift, however, my own cats sleep underneath it (as though it shelters them from rain), and I begin to lose patience.

"Come on, kitties," I trilled (at first). "Mmmm," I rubbed my cheek on the fleecy stuff. "Isn't this lovely? Wouldn't this make you feel like a—well, er, like an Eastern potentate, or a genie on a magic carpet, or a very fortunate cat having a nice lie-down suspended from a radiator?"

However, I stopped this approach after a week of failure. Now I pull on my thick gardening gloves, grab a wriggling cat by the waist, and hold it firmly on its new bed for about forty-five seconds until it breaks away.

I am reminded of a rather inadequate thing that men sometimes say to women, in an attempt to reassure them. The woman says, "I never know if you love me, Jonathan," and the man replies smoothly, "Well, I'm *here*, aren't I?" The subtext to this corny evasion (which fools nobody) is a very interesting cheat—it suggests that, should the slightest thing be wrong with this man's affections, he would of course push off immediately into the wintry night, rather than spend another minute compromising his integrity at the nice fireside with cups of tea.

Having a cat, I find, makes you susceptible to this line of reasoning—perhaps because it is your only direct line of consolation. "I wonder if he loves me," you think occasionally (perhaps as you search the doormat in vain for Valentines with paw prints on them). And then you gently lift the can opener from its velvet cushion in the soundproofed kitchen, and with a loud *ker-chunk-chunk* a cat comes cannoning through the cat flap, and skids backward across the linoleum on its bum. And you think cheerfully, "Well, of course he does. I mean, he's *here*, isn't he?"

Strutting the Catwalk:
Seven Habits of One Sexy Beast

Jennifer Jalalat

After polishing off a pint of chocolate chip cookie dough ice cream, I looked down at the roll that hung over the top of my jeans. For a minute, I sat there and thought about going for a jog.

I was still thinking about it when my cat, Dulcinea, slowly slunk her way into the center of the living room to demonstrate some kitty yoga. She began with a downward-facing dog and then took time to stretch out each leg behind her before finally flopping belly-up onto the floor, exposing her furry, portly middle while letting out a polysyllabic meow. I looked at her and realized that she was teaching me the first lesson in how to be a sexy beast:

1. Love what you've got. Even though any vet would tell you she's slightly overweight, Dulcinea wears those extra pounds with pride. Not sucking in at all, she shows off her assets and has a better body image than anyone I know. She is one fine feline and she knows it (and owns it).

After duly noting that she had a thing or three to teach me about embracing my sexy side, I started paying attention to other rules of the catwalk she might offer. Here's what I learned:

2. Make an entrance. When I have friends over, Dulcie's favorite thing to do is to arrive in a dramatic manner. She begins at the top of the stairs, acting nonchalant, and then gives herself a full body shake, making sure her black, white, and orange fur is all blended just how she likes it. Next, she runs down the stairs at full speed, calling out three big meows on her way down. Once she has everyone's attention, she makes her rounds, saying hello to each person in the room. Then she'll squeeze in, take a seat on the couch, and join the group, luxuriously stretching out her front right paw and resting it on someone who interests her. If she hasn't come down yet, my guests will ask where she is, but they should know that she runs on her own schedule. She'll be there when it suits her.

3. Always leave a mark. Whether it's her imprint on the top of the futon where she loves to nap or a fur print on the leg of my pants where she did a walk-by self-pet, I am constantly reminded of the presence of my glorious kitten. Clearly my cat is adept at leaving a mark, a subtle yet powerful technique in the craft of being a sexy beast.

4. Master the fine art of seduction. According to Dulcie, seduction occurs in the details. The delicately crossed paws. The slowly swinging tail. The half-closed, meditative eyes. The soft, low purr. She's got it down.

5. Expose your wild side. Dulcie endorses being one's own biggest fan, and not being afraid to let loose. She can get a little crazy, usually at night. She loves to chase her tail, roll around in catnip, and do mad soccer moves on her toy mice, never once thinking about how silly she might look.

6. Don't take yourself too seriously. Dulcie will walk up to me in complete seriousness, bumping my hand with her nose because she wants some attention, and the entire time one of her ears will be folded back like a bizarre piece of velveteen origami. She doesn't mind. Or her fur will be sticking up in a slight "faux mo" from the grooming that was interrupted by a short walk to her food bowl, just in case. During the summer, one of her favorite sleeping spots is a plant pot: She heaves all of her round furriness onto the top of a plant, shoving herself into the container. It looks ridiculous; her fur sticks out like a muffin top, but she loves it. She doesn't *care* how she looks.

Dulcinea

7. Celebrate your alone time.

Often when I come home from work, it's quite evident that Dulcie has been up to something. *What* she's been up to I'll never know, but it is clear that she has been basking in the greatness of being by herself. Maybe she's been chasing spiders, trying to get into her catnip, furring up my favorite black sweater, or just finishing up her twenty hours of beauty sleep. The point is, she fills up her alone time with stuff she loves to do. She certainly does not plant herself in front of the door and pine away for me, just waiting to see my face again. And the beautiful part about it is that when I am home and we are together, she really wants to be with me. Dulcinea is totally fulfilled with herself, yet happy to see me when I'm there.

She believes she's wonderful, and it's true. After all, when you strut around acting like you're a sexy creature, it doesn't take long before the feeling starts rubbing off on others.

Waiting for Fat Annie to Die. Not Really. Well, Sorta.

Barrie Gillies

My psychic lied to me. It happened when I was in my thirties and checking in with a palm reader—something I did a lot of back then. First she told me some exciting news: I was going to meet a great guy . . . finally! But then, things turned grave: She looked me in the eye and said, "Your cat will die. She knows she has to make room for your happiness. She knows you need to make space for this new man." Madame Zees-Your-Future went on to tell me that she knew I loved my cat, that she herself had cats, and that cats knew these things. Evidently, my cat, Fat Annie, knew she was standing (well, more like sprawling) between me and true love. So she was going to die so I could live happily ever after. And they say *dogs* are selfless!

Annie is twelve at the time. Not that old, but no frisky tabby, either. As far as I can tell, she doesn't show any signs of using up the last of her nine lives. And I show no signs of meeting Mr. Worth-Losing-My-Cat-Over. So Annie and I continue to coexist, two not-that-old-but-no-longer-kittenish roommates.

Don't get me wrong, it's not like I *want* her to die or anything. Eleven years earlier, I rescued Annie from a pound and I, a former

Fat Annie

Pekingese lover, instantly became a "cat person." No, I don't have cat sheets or notepads with little paw prints or framed photos of felines—Annie or otherwise—hanging on my walls. But people do gift me with goofy cat magnets, send me cat birthday cards, and buy me cat Christmas ornaments. (And I like them.) Annie's my best friend—she's seen me through countless bad breakups, she's shared my bologna and cheese sandwiches when I've come home too exhausted to even order out, and she curls up on my lap when I'm sad or sick or just watching a sappy movie. For my part, I put up with her 4:00 AM wake-up calls for snacks, her protest poops when I've committed some transgression like going away for the weekend, and her Garboesque pretensions (one shake of the Meow Mix box and she suddenly no longer vants to be alone). We've been "just us girls" for a long time, and I'm not ready to lose her. Besides, I don't believe in psychics anyway, really.

Several months after Madame Zees-Your-Future's grim prediction, I move. While three moving men haul my boxes between apartments in the July heat, I board Annie at the vet's. During a checkup, they find some mysterious fatty lumps. She needs an MRI right away. *So this is it*, I think to myself.

When I bring Fat Annie to our new home, we wait tensely for the results. Two days later: The fatty lumps are revealed to be . . . fatty lumps. Turns out, Fat Annie, who is fat, has fatty lumps on her fat. Phat.

That August I'm set up on a great blind date. Really. The guy is perfect—funny, cute, smart, solvent. Except he's allergic to cats. Itchy-scratchy-sneezy, uncomfortably, unbearably allergic. We don't spend much time at my apartment. Annie's dining solo more and more these days. When I do come home, she ignores me.

Fast-forward a year: a proposal, a wedding, a new home. Fat Annie isn't dead. Clearly, she has felt no need to make space for Mr. Worth-Losing-My-Cat-Over (MWLMCO). She's fourteen. She's still sleeping in the bed, sprawling on the couch, generally ruling the roost. I have made arrangements for her to live in the country with friends, but at the eleventh hour, MWLMCO breaks down— she can stay! He'll adjust.

"She'll die soon," I promise. "Thanks for letting her spend her last months with us."

"She looks fine to me," MWLMCO says.

"Trust me," I tell him, "she's a goner."

Fast-forward five more years. Fat Annie is still with us. I'm pregnant.

"I don't know how she's going to deal with a baby," MWLMCO mutters.

"She'll die. It won't be an issue," I answer. Secretly, I know Fat Annie, who's been my baby for eighteen years at this point, won't deal very well with this future adorable, helpless bundle of cuteness. She won't like it one bit, actually.

She'd better die.

Then, baby Will arrives and I'm terrified that I'll break this tiny tiny *tiny*—a third the size of Fat Annie!—baby. I keep Fat Annie totally away from Will. I ignore Annie. I shut her out of the bedroom. I'm scared Annie will claw Will, or hate him, or eat him. One day, I decide to see what will happen and we all sit in the living room together. I let Annie sniff Will. She walks away, disgusted. She is mad, but I can tell she won't eat him. I can tell she will never hurt Will. She'll just ignore him. He is nothing. She is everything. She is alive and well and still the queen of the household.

Will celebrates his first birthday. Fat Annie is now twenty years old. She is no longer fat; she's skinny, in fact. She has a little less pep in her prance. She spends most of her days under the bed or on the cool tiles next to the toilet, away from Will, who's learned the word "gentle" from petting the kitty, the few times he's run into her. We put Will to bed at eight or so, and Annie comes out of hiding, jumps on my lap, and allows me to scratch her. She knows she's still all that. And I'm glad the psychic lied. Sometimes you have to squish together to make room for a husband, a baby, a lot of happiness. And Fat Annie knew that, too.

Life with an Indian Street Cat

Sue Dickman

 For a time in my late twenties, I lived in an apartment in a residential, middle-class section of New Delhi. My landlord was an architect, and I lived on the middle floor of the house; the landlord's family lived on the ground floor, and his architectural office was on the top floor. Visitors needed to enter the gate at the front, walk up one flight of stairs to my terrace, and knock at the glass doors that opened into my living room.

The same was not true for cats.

A cat who wanted to come in could leap up onto the back wall from the alley behind the house, walk gingerly along the edge (which was lined with shards of broken glass to deter potential prowlers), and spring onto my back terrace. The back of my apartment faced the alley, and there was a tiny balcony off my bedroom, just big enough for a single chair. Sometimes, in good weather, I left the door open, and this became the second feline entrance.

I had been living in my apartment for several months before the first cat came—word must have gotten out in my neighborhood that the foreigner on the second floor was a soft touch. Keep in mind, Indians are not in the habit of keeping cats as pets; they consider them dirty and possibly dangerous. Street cats abound. I would see them scavenging in the garbage heaps, sometimes accompanied by canine—and even bovine—companions.

The first cat was brown and white, large for a street cat, with a loud voice and an affectionate nature. She turned up every few days, meowing loudly to make her presence known and then weaving between my legs, wanting attention. I thought of my parents' cat, Oliver, who came into their lives mewing pitifully in a snowstorm. (It was only weeks later that they learned he actually belonged to neighbors who had gone away on vacation.) I thought I would like to have a cat as part of my Indian life, especially a self-sufficient one. I was in India on a Fulbright scholarship, and while I traveled fairly often to do my research, there were also stretches when I was home for weeks at a time. Just when I was thinking that I wouldn't mind if cat number one decided to stay awhile, cat number two appeared. This one was scrawny, yellow, and entirely without charm. She was also possibly the most persistent cat I've ever met.

I was familiar with feline persistence. Oliver, after all, had returned to my parents' house daily, even after his owners were home again. He had decided that life with my parents would be a distinct improvement, and he made his preferences so clear that after a few months, the neighbors conceded defeat and brought over his basket and the rest of his food.

Ollie, however, had nothing on the scrawny yellow cat, who turned out to have an unpleasant and smarmy personality. At the beginning, I thought I had a choice. I thought that I could let the brown and white cat know that she was welcome and kick the smarmy one out often enough so she'd get my point. This seemed like a reasonable strategy. The first cat, however, knew differently. Each time she appeared, the smarmy cat followed almost immediately, meowing irritably and generally being unpleasant. Finally, the first cat stopped coming altogether, and the smarmy cat settled herself into my chair for a nap.

As the weeks passed, she morphed into Smarmo, and somehow, once she had a name (albeit a negative one), it meant that she was there to stay. She wasn't particularly clean, she wasn't particularly affectionate, she wasn't in any way the cat I would have chosen. I didn't feed her, didn't speak kindly to her. And yet she returned, day after day after day. I didn't actively make her leave, and she took that as license to stay. For several months we coexisted, Smarmo and I. We were both occupants of my apartment, but that didn't mean we were friends.

My landlords, meanwhile, were horrified by Smarmo's presence in my apartment. When the landlord's wife or mother

Smarmo &
Little Tavis

saw Smarmo walking across the wall to reach my back terrace, they shrieked as if they had found a rabid raccoon in their laundry basket. "It's only Smarmo," I tried to tell them, but they were not swayed. When my landlord's wife came upstairs to borrow my camera one day, she refused to come in because Smarmo was there (sleeping on the chair). She was convinced Smarmo would leap up and attack her if she came any closer, and I had to give her a camera lesson on the terrace with the door shut. Smarmo never moved from the chair.

Somehow, the landlords' dislike of Smarmo made me feel protective of her—maybe because they were not always thrilled with me, either. I was the first single woman they'd ever rented to, and they seemed to find me alarming. Admittedly, I was

living alone in a conservative, patriarchal country, and while
there were ways that I adapted, there were also ways I didn't—I
wanted a social life, for one. The grandmother—my most reliable
Hindi conversation partner—mostly wanted to talk about why
I wasn't married, and after a few of these chats, I did my best to
avoid them. My landlords were basically fine people, but I could
see how both Smarmo and I didn't fit into their worldview. It was
possibly our first bond.

It might have gone on like this indefinitely, this state of
feline/human détente, but then cat number three appeared. This
one was a black tomcat, and I saw him around the neighborhood,
lurking around the alley like a typical bad boy. Then I saw him
with Smarmo in a compromising position. Her scrawny body
swelled. One hot August night, monsoon season in Delhi, I heard
yowls coming from beneath my back terrace. In the morning, I
took a flashlight and shone it under the terrace. There, I found
Smarmo and a single kitten—a black and yellow calico with a
patch over one eye that gave her a raffish expression. I named the
kitten Tavis, Little Tavis for short.

This complicated things. Whatever my feelings (or lack
thereof) for Smarmo, she had given birth in my apartment. I kept
watch below the terrace, where Smarmo stayed, protectively
watching tiny Tavis. But early one morning, about a week after the

birth, I woke to a literal catfight going on in my bedroom. Smarmo crouched beneath my bed, hissing at the black tomcat who had strolled in. Sleepily, I tossed a paperback book—all I could find in the moment—in his direction, and he fled. When I was finally awake, I looked for Little Tavis, but she was gone. Of course I feared the worst. This was Delhi, where cats did not tend to come to good ends. "Tavis has been catnapped," I wrote sadly to my best friend, Becca.

Weeks passed. Smarmo continued to turn up, but there was no sign of Tavis. I had to assume she was gone. Smarmo remained her usual charmless self, and I thought that was that, at least until the black tomcat had his way with her again. But then one day I was working at my desk in my bedroom when Smarmo strolled through the door with something in her mouth. I didn't want to look at first—I thought it was a rat she had brought to eat in my apartment. But when I finally did look, I saw not a rat but none other than adorable-in-her-homeliness Little Tavis. It was as if Smarmo had moved her for her safety, but now that time had passed, she'd brought her back for a visit. I was delighted, and my feelings towards Smarmo softened the tiniest bit. Perhaps she wasn't such a terrible mother after all. "Tavis Found!!!" went out in the mail that afternoon.

After that, Smarmo brought Tavis over regularly. In her cat's mind, she had decided my apartment was safe again, and she seemed to look at me as some kind of kitten sitter. She'd bring Tavis over and leave her while she went to hunt. For her part, Tavis had reached the stage of adorable kittenhood, delighted by everything. She treated my apartment as her own private amusement park, swinging from my scarves, attempting to climb onto everything in sight. What could I do but go along with it?

My first nine months in Delhi had been a social whirlwind, but in the months after Tavis was born, it was quieter. Some of my friends had left for home, and it was the monsoon season, when not much goes on anyway. This was pre-Internet, so while I had a computer, it only served as a tool with which I could work. If I wanted to get in touch with a friend, I wrote a letter. If I was feeling extravagant, I faxed. So, there were nights I found myself home alone, dressed immodestly in the shorts and tank top I could only wear in my apartment, with nothing to do but hang out with Smarmo and Little Tavis. "This is what my life in Delhi has become," I wrote to my brother. "Here I am, hanging out with the street cats."

It made sense to me, though. One of the things I loved most about living in India was that I had a daily life, a routine. I was happy to have little chats in Hindi every morning with the guy at the vegetable stand, the man at the Mother Dairy milk stall, the boy in the market who knew exactly which newspapers I wanted to read (though he always tried to convince me to buy magazines with glossy photos of Bollywood stars instead). I loved it that the guy at the popcorn stand who set up outside the Bengali Sweet House in the nearby market expected my daily visit. I loved that I could shove my way onto the crowded buses, that I knew the routes and could read the Hindi on the signs. And when I came home again, grubby and tired, even if no friends were staying with me, I still had company.

In any case, it was hard not to be attached to Tavis. She was half street cat, half doted-on apartment cat. She was fierce, and then she sat in my lap and purred like an engine. "This is what cats do, Tavis," I'd tell her. "They sit on people's laps and get petted. It's okay if you like it." Because clearly, she was conflicted, and why wouldn't she be? Becca and I joked that when she was grown up, she would have to attend meetings for Adult Children of Street Cats. Becca even consulted with a friend about the possibility of bringing her back to the U.S. with one of us, but there were too many restrictions.

I have friends in Delhi now who have made a mission of rescuing street dogs. They have taken four large, affectionate, and docile dogs into their two-bedroom apartment, and they feed several more on the street. One of my friends, a dancer, gives benefit performances to raise money for street dog rescue, and he has coordinated the adoption of many dogs that otherwise would have lived their lives on the streets. My friends' dogs have won the equivalent of the street dog lottery.

I wonder, sometimes, if my apartment was a version of the cat lottery for Smarmo. She'd found someplace safe, someplace quiet, a haven from her usual life on the streets. I might not have doted on her, but I was probably the only person who tolerated her, who didn't shout at her or kick her or think she was dangerous. Perhaps if I'd met her before she became a hardened street cat, it would have been easier to love her. As it was, she became woven into the fabric of my life in Delhi. Everyone who visited me knew about Smarmo, a cat I didn't like, a cat who wouldn't go away. After a while, the fact that I didn't like her seemed beside the point.

After eighteen months in India, at the end of March 1995, I finally left. My friend Kathryn, who'd shared my apartment for my last month there, stayed on after I left. Smarmo, of course, also stayed put. I talked to Kathryn when she returned to the States six months later. Practically the first thing she mentioned was how she had gone to Kashmir and left the apartment locked and empty for three months, but within ten minutes of her return, Smarmo had turned up, waiting to be let in. I laughed so hard that I nearly wept. I was heartened and homesick all at once. Of course Smarmo had reappeared. We should have expected nothing less.

But there is a second ending to this story. I have been back to Delhi many times since 1995, although, with the exception of one awkward visit to my landlords' a few years later, I haven't returned to that apartment, or even to my old neighborhood. The year and a half I spent there is still precious to me, so even though I have watched India change each time I return, I don't want to see that neighborhood change. I want to think of it—and my life there—as it was. There is so much I still think about from that time—the wild group of expat friends I had, my travels all over the country doing research for my Fulbright project, the sweet, brief time I spent with the man who would later break my heart.

But I also have such a clear vision of myself in that apartment, the way the light came in from the alley into my bedroom, the sounds of the street in the early morning. I can see myself lying on my bedroom floor beneath the fan, listening to the BBC World Service on my little shortwave radio. It was the last time I felt so tangibly that I was ten thousand miles away from home. The Internet has changed everything, and somehow, the distance doesn't seem as much. It doesn't seem as dramatic anymore to spend such a long time, alone, in a foreign country. But, of course, I wasn't really alone at all. I had fabulous friends, and I had the cats, and that made all the difference.

The Cat from Oz
Kathryn Renner

Cats got a bad rap in my childhood.

"They jump up on counters around food." My mother could barely form the thought without gagging. When I was twelve, I thought I'd see for myself what this cat thing was all about by baby-sitting for a family with two indoor cats. Who knew I would have an allergic fit? My eyes deteriorated into slits; my arms and legs morphed into a patchwork of angry splotches. There was no love lost between me and those furballs. Besides, I adored Spooker, a perky blue-breasted parakeet unveiled on my Halloween birthday, and didn't cats bat birds around before finishing them off?

Even though I grew up in a religious family devoted to prayer and loving our brethren, our earth, and all creatures, it didn't occur to me to see those counter-prowling predators—the ones who preferred our flower beds over the litter boxes their owners would scoop, the ones who grinned over a defeathered bird snatched near the feeder—in a more compassionate light. For the sake of my nasal passages and epidermis, I stayed well enough away.

Until years later . . . when a cat came to me like a hymn.

Long after Spooker's last tweet, I was working at the kitchen sink of my own first home when I heard tires squeal outside. I looked up in time to see a blond and white short-haired cat thrown from a car window before the rusted-out beater with sagging exhaust pipe sped away. And there, having landed deftly in the grass on all fours, stood my next prayer mission. Maybe I could have overlooked praying for a pesky cat, but I could not shrug off such cruelty. So the seek-and-ye-shall-find instinct kicked in. When in need, when in crisis, when an unscheduled cat arrives thrust from a passing car, consult the Big Guy.

Dear God, I know you wouldn't create a rat fink person who would abandon this animal—a pretty raunchy-looking one, I might add, dear Father. All Seeing, you know this creature makes me wheeze and scratch. Spare my kitchen counters and the hygiene of my food. Protect the goldfinches at my feeder. But may some poor sap take in this wretched beast. Amen.

For days I spotted the abandoned cat on neighbors' window-sills, rubbing against screens and fixing pitiful, laser green eyes on any passing human. As much as I abhorred how someone could just discard an animal, I would not break down and adopt this rogue. If it were a dog, maybe. But a cat . . . I could not . . . I *would* not.

But you don't have to be a cat person to understand the language of starvation. Meows escalated into yowls. To make matters worse, it was the week of Thanksgiving: With the pervading scent of roasting turkey and pumpkin pies, my side porch right off the kitchen became the chosen venue for a kitty meltdown. This time the Big Guy suggested I talk to the beast directly:

All right, just one gizzard, you pathetic creature. Let me crack open the door just a sliver . . . no, you're not coming in here, Buster! I'm holding you back with my foot, see? This is no love offering . . . I'm just going to fling this sucker yonder by the fence. There, eat and then go find a home, cat. Amen.

So it was a gizzard here, a scrap of dark meat there, all tossed in an overhand arc that kept the urchin rushing to the fence and boomeranging back. And it was during one of those remote visitations that I glimpsed what made me, as a daily reader of the Good Word, a little more interested in this cat's salvation. It had a tumor—definitely, a knotty lump on its stomach. This cat was sick. Some slimeball threw this cat away rather than deal with its affliction.

I named her (after investigating, definitely a her) Toto, hoping the moniker might make her more doglike. And besides, tossed through the air into her new situation, she sure as heck wasn't in

Toto

Kansas anymore. Who knew where she came from? But she knew exactly where she was going. In short order she graduated from the porch to the garage to the laundry room and was soon draped over the sofa like an afghan. Every time I touched her I ran to wash my hands before I erupted like Mount

Vesuvius into a poster child for antihistamines.

Although I was surprised by the affection simmering between me and this cat, I mainly had a mission. I had to heal Toto's tumor. Still steeped in the faith healing of my religious upbringing, I had never been to a doctor, so taking her to a vet didn't occur to me. Toto was catapulted into a clan treated solely with the metaphysical. Not to worry: Hadn't prayer pulled me through whooping cough, measles, strep throat, and menstrual cramps? Wasn't it prayer that had led me to lost keys, a matching end table after the style was discontinued, a parking place at the mall during year-end sales? With a roof over her head, a bath, and a steady diet of Fancy Feast, Toto—though inherently dainty and slight—became robust. Unfortunately, so did her tumor.

OK, Lord, your humble servant knows that when you let this cat out of the original bag it was healthy and perfect, so shouldn't it be now? You being Head Cat Kahuna, you who have no allergies and never itch, hold this cat in your light and let it be whole. Amen.

It was a few more weeks before my supplications were answered. Not with any flash of lightning or laying on of hands: The revelation came when Toto returned from a day of investigating neighbors' yards and fishponds. That night, with the TV blaring and Toto stretched out next to me on the sofa, I reached over to pet her and felt something odd around her collar.

There, taped to her new ID tag, was a small piece of tightly rolled paper. A secret message? I peeled it off and unwound a note written in black ballpoint pen:

"Call us when the kittens come. We'd love to have one! 619-555-1000."

Two weeks later, seven healthy kittens were born near the washing machine, in a box lined with bright Garfield beach towels. Toto could barely lift her head; she was spent after all that birthing. Still, her eyes wouldn't leave those babies. There was never a better mother. Watching her clean, feed, and protect them, watching her intuit which was the weakest and needed the most care, was indeed a testament to a Higher Power. And a few weeks after the last weaned kitten was given away to a grateful owner, Toto and I stepped over the threshold of medicine, first entering the world of a vet to get her spayed, then off to an allergist for me. There was no turning back.

Uh, God, you didn't tell me that doctors were so useful. Thank you for putting them on your earth. And cats . . . I can see why you made them, too. Toto sends regards. Amen.

Not that Toto needing to get fixed was the ultimate epiphany that changed my religious persuasions. But it was a step, a peek from the cloistered teachings I had taken for granted. Over time, I would shed my childhood religion, editing out what no longer made sense and honoring my own faith in something bigger than myself—a mystical, loving GPS device for a lost cat or willful soul.

Toto lived with me for twelve years, through marriage, three house moves and the birth of my own two babies. An obedient pet, in time she did become more doglike. She followed us on neighborhood walks, parked herself like a sentry in the driveway to watch for our approaching car, and played a mean game of hide-and-seek. And when my small children cried, she rose from her deep sleep in the sun, came to their side, and gently put one paw on their laps, as caring and concerned as the Darling family's Saint Bernard nursemaid in *Peter Pan*.

She never stopped grinning about nabbing the occasional bird at the feeder or lizard sprawled comatose on a sun-baked tile on our Southern California patio. The remains left on our stoop, offered as gifts, left my softhearted children sobbing over the demise. But in the end we forgave this transgression. After all, wasn't Toto's road to my door navigated by an omnipotent Oz? She came with brains, courage, and heart and dropped in on a mission, just where she was meant to be.

Call Me Crazy . . .
My Life as a Cat Lady

Lisa L. Goldstein

I still remember the moment I started to doubt my sanity when it came to cats: It was in the early '90s, when I adopted my second one. I had called my mother with the news, and her reaction came as a surprise: She cried.

Maybe if I start at the beginning, you'll understand why she was so emotional. You see, I wasn't always crazy about cats. In fact, once upon a time, when I was a little girl back in the '60s, I feared and disliked cats, feelings based on scary "cat creature" stories told to me, in all innocence, by my mom. Fast-forward to a house party in a Brooklyn brownstone circa 1985. I'm sitting in a chair, talking to some people, when the resident Siamese cat jumps onto my lap, settles into the Sphinx position, and remains there for the rest of the evening, purring and giving me a look that is downright loving. Strangely, not only am I not afraid, I'm actually charmed.

That creature must've been a supernatural ambassador from the feline netherworld, on a mission to convert a new cat person or something. I'm not exactly sure what she did to me (except offer more sweetness and affection than I would have expected to receive on a random Saturday evening out in the '80s), but I felt that something magical happened to me that night. Afterward, I couldn't stop thinking about that cat, and I came to realize that I had unfairly maligned and misunderstood the entire feline species all those years. It wasn't long before I developed an intense curiosity about all I'd been missing in the cat world.

So I went to the ASPCA a few times—just to look, I told myself. But I think you can already see where this story is going. Inevitably, I adopted a sweet black cat I named Snooky. She and I were best pals from the start, and we became emotionally inseparable. I slept better when she slept next to me. When she developed the sniffles or an infected tooth, I worried and suffered, too. If I was sad, she was empathetic. Once, when I was having an argument on the phone, she became so distressed at hearing me raise my voice that she jumped up onto the table next to me and poked the receiver out of my hand. Her mere presence comforted me.

Within a few weeks of bringing Snooky home, I was back at the ASPCA, but not to adopt another cat. I felt compelled to visit the cats that I hadn't "rescued" when I chose Snooky, and I soon decided to volunteer at the shelter. In reality, though, as much as my desire to volunteer came from an altruistic impulse, I had to admit that, where cats were concerned, I really just wanted to be around them.

After about a year of volunteering, I adopted another black cat I named Henry (after Henry Bergh, the founder of the ASPCA). That's what prompted my mom to cry. I couldn't imagine what was so disturbing about my having two cats, but it was clear she wasn't weeping for joy.

"I see all your friends getting married," she explained, "and I don't see you making an effort to meet people. I'm afraid that you're going to get completely involved with your cats, and they'll become your whole life." Given that my mom has never been particularly desperate to see me get married, it was disconcerting to hear her so concerned over me sharing my life with a cat or two, and equating it with my potential to become a lonely freak. I think I can pinpoint that as the first moment anyone feared that I might become a crazy cat lady.

Her reaction got me thinking, though: What *is* a crazy cat lady, anyway? So I did a little digging. According to

UrbanDictionary.com, the common definition is "A woman, usually middle-aged or older, who lives alone with no husband or boyfriend, and fills the empty, lonely void in her life with as many cats as she can collect in one place."

We've all seen news stories about people like this: Women who are found to have dozens (or, in extreme cases, hundreds) of

Henry

cats roaming around their homes in various states of filth and poor health, after neighbors have complained about the stench. I always imagined these women to be unbalanced but kindhearted people who started out with the most admirable motivation, to care for animals that would otherwise be living on the street, or worse. But somehow they ended up warehousing the animals, never thinking, "Hmmm, maybe I have one (or thirty-five) too many." Hence, the authentic crazy cat lady.

Is there a psychological profile for women who collect cats? To study this phenomenon, among others, the Hoarding of Animals Research Consortium (HARC) was formed in 1996. They've found that women are most likely to accumulate cats (while men more frequently collect dogs), that hoarding is a symptom of obsessive-compulsive disorder, that approximately two-thirds of hoarders are women, and, not surprisingly, that 70 percent of them are unmarried. Social isolation is common among women who fit the profile, though, interestingly, experts believe it's a *result* of the hoarding behavior rather than the cause of it.

But perhaps the most intriguing aspect of these people's common experience is that, typically, animals played a significant role in their childhoods, which were often described as chaotic with unstable parenting. Their difficult childhoods set them up to have problems establishing close human connections in adulthood. So they grow up to surround themselves with animals, which provide them with the emotional comfort they need. In this context, these people are comfortable only in the insulated world they've created at home—a utopia where there's unconditional, unquestioning love from cats.

There may also be a scientific explanation for why people with even a few cats are perceived as being "different." A study reported in August 2006 revealed that a parasitic microbe commonly found in cats might actually manipulate the personalities of infected people. According to Kevin Lafferty, a U.S. Geological Survey scientist at the University of California, Santa Barbara, infection by *Toxoplasma gondii* can make some people more prone to anxiety, insecurity, or depression. Interestingly, the microbe is thought to have different, and often opposite, effects on men versus women, but both genders appear to develop a form of neuroticism called "guilt proneness" after being infected by the parasite. Could that be why some women become willing servants to the many cats in their lives—assigning them priority over boyfriends, careers, friends, and family—whereas men merely cohabitate with a kitty or two and otherwise continue to lead normal lives?

No matter what the root cause, there you have both a profile of the classic, animal-hoarding crazy cat lady, and a scientific theory explaining how a cat can come into a person's life and take over her mind (as well as the best spot on her bed, her comfy living room chair, every windowsill, and any folded newspaper that a person.might want to read). But what does all this have to do with me, a gal with two cats? I decided to find out.

A friend recently asked what I consider to be my Achilles heel. I answered that although I'm not afraid of much, I live in fear of being judged. Nevertheless, I'll divulge that I actually have three cats now. Usually when I meet new people, I postpone that revelation for as long as possible, and I think you can guess why. When a single woman has one or two cats, she's considered relatively normal, but if she takes on three or more, society is quick to lump her in with the women who don't know how many is too many. And from there, the assumption is that she's destined to remain unmarried, to neglect her health, hygiene, and living conditions, and, eventually, to stop leaving her house altogether.

Why does a single woman with a bunch of cats spell "social outcast," whereas a single woman with dogs is usually thought to be generous and kindhearted? Maybe society views women with dogs differently because the assumption is that canines force a person to venture outdoors twice a day (after all, you've got to walk them). A woman with cats, on the other hand, can have thirty-pound bags of litter and cases of canned cat food delivered to her home, and can in theory avoid having interaction with anyone who doesn't answer to the likes of "Fluffy" or "Tiger." (Once she reaches that stage, of course, it's probably for the best that she *doesn't* venture into the real world, because the people in it are bound to judge her.)

Case in point (and speaking of people judging): A few years ago I went on a blind date, and after the guy had looked me over a couple of times (don't ask), he declared, "You're not what I was expecting for a woman with three cats." When I asked what he had envisioned, he answered, "Overweight and sloppy," without hesitation. It was hard to accept that anyone could be so proud to endorse such an unfair stereotype. Not surprisingly, that was our first and last date.

Is there something inherently wrong with having more than two cats? And am I really a crazy cat lady because I have three? I decided to ask around.

First, **I asked a sociologist.** Doctoral student Alison Hatch is a graduate part-time instructor in the department of sociology at the University of Colorado at Boulder. She believes the "crazy cat lady" stigma parallels the age-old concern about women who haven't settled down with a man by a certain age. The single woman with multiple cats is thought to be exchanging cat companionship for male companionship, she says. The woman is committing to take care of multiple felines, but not to put her energy into looking after a man, and this raises eyebrows in society. And since we "gender" companion animals (in that cats are seen as feminine animals, and dogs as masculine animals), we assume that a woman with multiple cats will never find a man who'd be willing to live with all that feminine energy. Thus, in choosing to have cats, she has doomed herself to the life of a "spinster."

Of course, Ms. Hatch is quick to point out that this is all a stereotype, given the fact that (1) plenty of both women and men have multiple cats and aren't anywhere near clinically insane, and (2) society rarely assigns the "crazy cat lady" label to the married woman who has multiple cats, apparently because she is not a threat to our social expectations.

Lisa L. Goldstein

Excellent—I could blame society for the prejudice against women who love cats. I was comfortable with that.

Still, I thought I'd seek a second opinion, so **I asked my therapist,** whom I've always considered to be the voice of reason. His view was that because of movies, fairy tales, and other cultural influences, the cat has historically been viewed as the ultimate symbol of femininity (even though, obviously, there are both male and female felines). The image of a woman in a house with cats is, in a positive sense, a maternal image of warmth, but society assumes that her cats are the only creatures she's willing to have relationships with, so she becomes the "crazy cat lady."

So, from this perspective, it's once again society that is messed up—there's nothing necessarily wrong with the cat ladies themselves. I felt good about hearing this conclusion from an unbiased medical professional.

Talking to experts is all well and good, but in order to get the real story, I had to ask single men. After all, they're the ones who have the most clearly defined deal-breakers about women, and I was sure they could offer some no-holds-barred opinions. So **I asked a group of (extremely) random single guys of varying ages and descriptions on Match.com.** My highly unscientific poll revealed the following: There are a lot of guys out there who (1) don't like cats, (2) don't understand cats, (3) don't understand the relationship between women and cats, and (4) don't want to answer questions about cats, but will answer them anyway if they think it might lead to a date with a relatively attractive woman. In other news, I also learned that there are many men out there who—aside from being slightly prejudiced against cats—are inarticulate and not terribly bright. But that's a story for another day. Here are some responses about how many cats are too many in a woman's life:

"One cat, I get. Two, they have each other for companionship. Why would a woman need more than two?"

"I think after two it's kind of weird. I think if you like cats and want to have two so they have company that's okay. Three seems obsessive. That being said, if I found a woman beautiful, smart, funny, and generally interesting, I would deal with any amount of cats. Heck, she could have guinea pigs, mice, and fish and I would deal with it."

"More than two cats would seem strange, but more than four would start turning me off, as I think that person needs to better focus her interests. I like animals, but I prefer humans to animals. For instance, I would not be turned off if a woman had many children."

"Three is the cutoff. More than that indicates the person may be too into animals at the expense of people/relationships. Plus, these furry creatures invariably want to come inside when they're outside, and vice versa. Acting as a doorman for a few is fine, but if it becomes a full-time job, I'll pass."

"Anything more than three cats would become an issue. I like cats, but too much of a good thing can be bad. I'm a huge dog person, and if a woman had four dogs, even *that* would be too much for me."

"I'm not sure I understand the question."

"So, would you like to get together sometime to see if there is chemistry between us?"

Yikes! My worst fears about having three cats were confirmed: Even if a man was willing to date me, he'd likely be harboring the suspicion that I was "too into" my four-legged cohorts, or that they'd ruin any chance of us having a good sex life, or—worst of all—that I wouldn't have any love left for him, after lavishing it on my companion animals 24–7.

But I still wasn't sure I had the full picture, so **I asked my mom** to chime in. I knew she'd have an opinion on the subject, given her visceral reaction when I adopted Henry. Her thinking was simple: A woman has two hands; therefore she can easily handle two cats. But once she gets beyond that number, it's like trying to juggle three balls at once—it becomes a feat of coordination. Plus, three cats require that much more devotion—

you don't want one to feel less loved than another (spoken like the mother of three kids, Mom!)—so each one's needs become your preoccupation. Also (and this is key), once you realize you can handle three, you think, What's keeping me from having four? And then why stop there?

Admittedly, my mom has her own personal bias. So **I asked my close friend Anne,** who also just so happens to be one of the smartest, most insightful people I know, for her opinion. Her feeling is that guys feel overpowered when a woman has more than two cats. "When there are two cats, it's a cats-equals-humans equation," she said. "When there are three cats, though, the guy has one more cat in the vicinity that he needs to keep an eye on. Plus, when there are three cats, there's a greater chance that one of them will be totally psycho and prone to clawing a guy while he sleeps, or peeing on his clothes."

The bottom line, she said, is that guys see cats as the dangerous, mystical aspect of women, and that they can generally control their fear as long as they don't have to deal with more than one or two. Beyond that, they may feel that women are aligning themselves with a tribe of aloof, self-sufficient felines.

Having gotten all that input on the subject from outsiders, I had no choice but to look at myself and ask, honestly, "Am I a crazy cat lady?" And, if not, "Am I on the verge of becoming one?"

Lisa L. Goldstein

I didn't even *want* three cats originally: After I adopted Henry in 1992, I had set my cat limit at two. I told myself it was best to restrict the amount of cat hair (and litter box changes and tears from my mother) that comes with the multiple-cat lifestyle. In the back of my mind, though, I wondered whether I had drawn the line at two because I was afraid of getting too close to crazy cat lady land. Even for me, three seemed like the gateway to who knows how many. And let's face it: You never hear of people going back to only two or four or nine cats once they've had several dozen; they just drift further and further from reality and society.

After Snooky passed away in 2000, Henry seemed lonely (as was I), so I agreed to foster a little gray cat from Animal Haven, the shelter where I was volunteering in Queens. She had been abused—and almost killed—by a group of teenage boys, and was recovering from her injuries in a cage, which was far from ideal for her, both physically and psychologically. When I brought her home, she and Henry became fast friends, and I decided to adopt her officially. I named her Lily, after the lily of the valley, the flower that represents the return of happiness.

The following year, after September 11, New York City's animal shelters were brimming with feline refugees from Ground Zero. During those days, the feeling among New Yorkers was that everyone needed to help get the city back on its feet. So I decided to break my own two-cat rule and adopt a 9/11 orphan. But before I got the chance, I came across a handicapped kitten at Animal Haven. A little white cat with gray markings, she was suffering from cerebellar hypoplasia, a condition that affected her ability to control her movements. When I first saw her, she was trying to stand up in her cage, but she trembled so badly that she kept

Daisy

falling over. When I took her out of her cage, she relaxed in my arms and fell asleep in about seven seconds.

I knew that most potential adopters wouldn't give this cat a second look. And since so many people had come into the shelter specifically for animals that had been rescued after the terrorist attacks, I knew there would be plenty of good homes for those cats. So I adopted the kitten and named her Daisy, after the flower that represents innocence.

Once I adopted Daisy, however, I found myself seeking a reality check from my therapist, to see if I was entering dangerous territory. I asked him whether the number of cats under my care could impact my need (or lack of need) for human companionship. I should mention that at this point I hadn't had a relationship in several years. Yes, I dated occasionally, but I never seemed to meet the right guy. So I was already afraid that I preferred cats to people, and that I was, at heart, a freakish loner. My therapist's opinion, however, was that my affinity for cats and my avoiding relationships with men were separate issues.

By adopting Daisy, I was trying to give her the chance she deserved at a good life. But I couldn't shake the feeling that I, like other lonely people, had gravitated toward cats because they're fiercely independent, and therefore if they accept you into their world, you really, *really* feel loved. Or maybe I was looking for the kind of acceptance I wasn't finding with males of the human species, who I often felt misunderstood me. I also had to question whether, over time, cats were destined to replace the men I might have had in my life—not because I couldn't tear myself away from my feline-filled apartment long enough to go on a date, but because I had become so accustomed to cats' unconditional love and their lack of judgment and criticism that, somewhere along the line, the idea of participating in an actual relationship with a man had begun to seem almost messy and burdensome by comparison. Hard to admit, but true.

For the record, I'm crazy about men, and I also adore dogs. (See? Plenty of love to go around!) And I should point out that I've spent over fourteen years volunteering at animal shelters, and in that time there have been many cats I've wished I could save.

So imagine all the cats I could have taken home, but didn't. If I were *really* crazy, I would have found a way to justify each new adoption, and I'd be living with about fifteen felines now.

Still, the question remains: Has my mom's fear come to fruition? Have I become a crazy cat lady after all? I offer the following facts for your consideration:

Lily

1. I'm unmarried at age forty-five (though I believe it's my philosophical objections to the institution of marriage that have kept me from taking the plunge), and I share my home with three cats.

2. A few years ago I ordered a set of wooden bunk beds for the cats. I figured Daisy, with her handicap, could crawl into the lower bunk without too much trouble, and the other two kitties would enjoy perching on the top bunk to survey their surroundings. Then, in full Martha Stewart mode, I made flannel sheets and fleece pillowcases for the beds, because I knew it would make the kitties cozy and happy, which it did. And that made *me* happy. Uh-oh.

3. If I was blindfolded and someone held each of my cats up to my face, I could identify each by the smell of its breath.

Okay, I know what you're thinking: *Cuckoo!* So sue me—I

have three cats and I love them as if they were my children. Is my situation mitigated by the fact that my apartment is clean, my furniture is not covered with cat hair, and you can't smell the litter box, even if you're standing right next to it? Does that change your opinion? How about the fact that I socialize with friends, go to the gym regularly, and date men whenever a good one comes along? Am I a crazy cat lady? Maybe or maybe not; it depends whom you ask. Just don't ask me—apparently when you actually become one, you're the last to know.

A Muse in Training

Carol Driscoll

Elizabeth Barrett Browning had a speckled spaniel named Flush. John Steinbeck traveled the country with a standard poodle named Charlie, and the novelist Colette always had a cat by her side when she wrote. Taking their cue, I decided that a hardworking and isolated freelance writer like me also needed a pet, so I adopted a kitten at the local animal shelter.

What I hoped for was a feline companion sitting by my side while I wrote—a presence that somehow affirmed and approved of my painstaking literary labors.

What I got instead was a six-month-old ginger tabby whose skills as a silent and supportive collaborator are sketchy, to say the least.

I named him Huck Finn, and like his namesake, he's

rebellious and independent. Finn prefers constant movement rather than the inaction of a calm, sedentary sage. When the printer begins its noisy process, he jumps into the paper tray to investigate the source of the clatter. He prances back and forth across the keyboard the minute I lean back to ponder my next word. He is curious about the complex wiring hooked to my

Huck Finn

computer and monitor, and I need to remove him from the nest of cables under my desk at least five times a day. If I become too intent on my work, he climbs onto me using each tiny, needlelike claw as he goes, and purrs softly into my ear. I have learned how to walk with a kitten on my ankle and how to type with one hand (and insert the uppercase letters and fix the mangled punctuation later) while I hold him with the other. If he gives up on getting my full attention while I write, he gets it when I have to clean up the shattered glasses and cups he's knocked from the countertop or reroll the toilet paper he has unwound onto the bathroom floor.

But after two months, I'm happy to report that there are signs of improvement. For one thing, he's able to settle down for short periods of time while I write. During these brief spurts of inactivity,

I question him on the finer points of what I'm writing. "Do you think the second paragraph should be the lead paragraph?" He looks up at me, his face positioned between his paws, his lengthening body stretched to the max. I take that as a yes. When the first draft is finished, I read it aloud to him. He yawns twice, rakes his tongue through his fur for a thorough grooming, stretches, circles, and turns away from me to face the wall.

"Tough crowd," I mutter to myself.

Maybe it will take many more "readings" to awaken his literary skills, but I'm afraid that muses, much like writers, are born, not made. Or perhaps I've been at the computer too long and just need to get some fresh air. I will do that right after I pull Finn out of an open hanging file.

Lessons Learned
from a Blind Cat

Linda Kay Hardie

I felt sorry for myself when the vet told me my favorite cat, Rudy, needed eye surgery. Her corneas had growths on them, which needed to be removed or they would rupture. The surgery had to be done immediately, because the cat eye doc wouldn't be back in town for another month.

Rudy, a five-year-old fawn Abyssinian, had always been active. Her trademark was a piercing cry as she dropped a wrapped after-dinner mint at my feet, her demand for a game of fetch. Although middle-aged for a cat, she still rocketed through the house at lightning speed.

It was tough to condemn this dynamic cat to blindness, even for just a week. How was I going to care for a blind cat in a household of five active cats?

And how could I afford this?

The doctor assured me that the surgery was straightforward. Just a slice across the corneas to remove the growths, then a quick stitching to hold the eyelids closed for a week as the corneas healed. Plus a plastic funnel collar to keep Rudy from scratching out the stitches.

I anticipated a hard week. Cats are sensitive to weakness and adjust their hierarchy quickly. Rudy had always considered herself top cat of the household, and I feared that her blindness would encourage a coup. I pictured myself becoming her "seeing eye person" to protect her from the other cats.

When I picked her up, Rudy was still groggy from the anesthetic. "Keep her confined for a while," the vet assistant advised.

Fat chance.

I'd planned to leave Rudy in the carrier for an hour to let the other cats get used to her. She howled. I compromised. I took the carrier into my bedroom and closed the other cats out. I put Rudy on my bed and talked to her, to help her get used to being blind.

Not good enough. She flopped off the bed immediately and marched toward the door. I grabbed her and put her back on the bed. She hopped down and stomped away again. This time I walked in front of her, talking so she could follow my voice. She refused to stay locked in my room. Rudy began to find her way almost immediately. As she wandered through the house, obviously searching for something, I realized it had to be the litter box. I called to her from the bathroom, where the box sits in the tub. She confidently marched in. I lifted her into the bathtub and put her paws in the litter. By the second day, she'd found her way to the bathroom and into the box without guidance.

I took her for walks in the back yard. Sometimes she sat in the dirt, a compact loaf of a cat, just listening. Other times she roamed around, cautiously looking for excitement. Rudy loved trouble. Inside or out, she always knew when one of the non-Aby cats was nearby. She stalked up to Mollie and Chipper, my mixed-breed cats—who were transfixed by her blindness—and hissed loudly. She was determined to be queen of the household, even blind.

She accepted hand-feeding only because I fed her bites of fresh, home-cooked turkey breast, her favorite treat. But she wanted dry food and water set up so she could feed herself on her own schedule.

After a full day of watching out for her, it was clear that Rudy wasn't the invalid I had expected her to be. She devised her own system for getting around—she used the funnel collar as a white cane. The plastic sides of the collar were long enough to protect her face, so this spirited cat marched through the house, expecting to find walls and furniture by bumping into them. It was like an extra-long, sturdier set of whiskers.

Rudy could perceive light and dark through her eyelids, which helped her tell when someone approached. She could also hear differences in the sound quality of each room, apparently relying on echoes to help her figure out where anyone was.

Rudy

I knew this because I began to hear the difference between rooms, too. The bathroom had an echo to it, even in silence. The living room, with couch and chairs and drapes and rug, had a heavier feel. I began remembering where I'd left things, rather than assuming I could just glance around for them.

Rudy had no way of knowing that her blindness was only temporary. She just accepted it and learned to work with what she had. I felt ashamed that my biggest worry about the surgery had been what it would cost and how it would inconvenience me.

At the end of the week, Rudy continued to push her limits. While I was working at my desk, she climbed onto my telephone table, then onto my desk, and from there she tried to find her way onto the filing cabinet. I tapped on top of the cabinet to remind her where it was. She pulled her way up there, then up onto the bookshelf above. She always loved heights, and she wasn't about to let blindness stop her, even if she couldn't see the view.

Rudy went through a total of five eye surgeries. I stopped counting the cost when it hit $4,500. The final surgery came after one of her eyeballs ruptured. She'd simply run out of cornea from all the surgeries. The doctor said if Rudy were a person, she'd be legally blind.

When I clipped the stitches after the requisite week this last time, I could see that Rudy was upset. Angry. After previous surgeries, she'd had perfect vision again once the stitches came out. Not this time. This time, she would only have partial vision in one eye.

Rudy shook her head. She blinked her eyes. Her whole body stiffened. She stalked off to hide under the bed, refusing to acknowledge my existence.

The next day, I heard a *clunk* from my bedroom. I ran out of my office, worried Rudy had fallen off something. I searched for the source of the noise. Finally I looked up. There, on top of the six-foot-tall entertainment center, was my blind cat. I later observed how she did it. With vision, such as it was, in only one eye, Rudy would scrunch her neck down and look at the object she wanted to leap onto. Then she would stretch her neck out long.

Instead of the everyday depth perception we all use, thanks to two working eyes side by side, Rudy was faking it with her one eye. She never missed.

Rudy lived for ten years with her blindness. She could sense shadows and light well enough to avoid boxes and furniture. I never worried about setting down a grocery bag, because I knew she wouldn't run into it. She had no problem coping with several house moves.

She spent much of her time up on top of high places: the entertainment center, the refrigerator. In one apartment, there wasn't a counter close enough to the fridge. Rudy kept trying, but the leap was just too far. I had to put a short bookcase in the kitchen, between the counter and the fridge, so that she could make the leap, because I could tell she wasn't going to give up trying.

Cancer finally claimed her life. Rudy fought that, too, but eventually she'd had enough.

To this day, I can't help but remember lessons that Rudy taught me. She made me realize that we're all only as handicapped as we act. We set our own limitations. If we want to climb a hill whose boundaries we don't know—and for a view we can't even see—all we need to do is try.

Linda Kay Hardie

Hold Me!
Touch Me! Love Me!
(a.k.a. the Story of Sophie)

Heather Gowen Walsh

"Don't worry, you probably won't even see her except when you put out food."

That was my big introduction to Sophie the cat. I was going through a midtwenties funk and, in a quest to find meaning in my life (beyond going to work and then out to happy hour), had started volunteering at an animal shelter. I was excited to be there—or at least to be involved with the dogs there. After all, I'd cared for dogs all my life. The cat part, however . . . not so much. I just wasn't a cat person—cats actually kinda weirded me out with their shrill meowing and tendency to attack first, ask questions later.

Then one day I got a call. The shelter had just taken in a cat that wasn't doing so hot being surrounded by hundreds of other cats. Could I take her home for two weeks so she could get a little peace and quiet? After some hemming and hawing (and checking with my two roommates), I agreed.

"Great," said the volunteer coordinator on the phone. "It'll be easy—cats do their own thing and tend to hide out from their owners. I doubt you'll see her at all."

She then went on to recount what they knew about the cat: Someone had left her in a bag on the front steps of the shelter. Her fur was so matted that they couldn't get a brush through it and had to completely shave her, and her claws had grown so long that they were curling over, piercing the pads on her paws. Plus, she was skinny—six pounds, tops.

Still, this description didn't quite prepare me for my first introduction to Sophie. For starters, I thought she would look like a normal cat—you know, the kind on Meow Mix commercials. But she was a Persian, complete with scrunched-up face and lots of wheezing noises. The shave job didn't help her appearance, nor did the brown discharge oozing from her eyes and nose (more on that later).

But I had made a promise, so I took her home. And, sure enough, Sophie made a break for it the minute I let her out of the carrier and shot directly under my bed. I didn't see or hear from her for the next six hours.

This'll be a piece of cake, I thought.

Cut to the middle of the night. I woke up to realize that I had six pounds of stinky cat sitting on my chest, staring at me. Then she walked around to the top of my head and started pawing at my hair. I later found out that kneading is common among cats—but that night, as she slowly teased my hair into something similar to a beehive, I thought this cat had lost her mind. It kind of felt good, though, and I eventually dozed off. When I woke up that morning, she was cuddled next to me on the pillow.

And so began life with an affection-whore for a pet. For the next two weeks, Sophie couldn't get enough of me. If I was home, she was on my lap—or in my hair. I'd wake up at night to find her spooning me—or pawing at my arm to spoon her. She wasn't happy unless she was kneading my chest, my lap, my neck, even if it meant her claws were shredding my clothes to bits.

After two weeks, there was no way I could send her back to shelter life. She'd become my baby—albeit a starved-for-attention, very demanding baby. I signed the adoption papers and set about giving Sophie the happy home she'd obviously never had.

Of course, my roommates were less than thrilled. For starters, Sophie had no problem attempting to knead their hair—or clothes, or blankets, or rugs—when I wasn't home. And let's face it, cat litter in a small apartment is just gross and smelly, no matter how often you change it. To top it off, Sophie's oozing eyes and nose were leaving brown marks all over our walls and furniture. I was spending crazy money on vets and prescriptions, but nothing seemed to stop the problem. Despite this, we all managed to get along for a few months.

Then the sneezing began. Not me, not Sophie, but one of my roommates. After a few trips to the doctor, it was determined that

Sophie

Sophie was the cause. I didn't know what to do—I couldn't get rid of her, and, having signed my life away on the lease, I couldn't just move out and get a new apartment. And that, my friends, is when my kinda-sorta boyfriend at the time made an offer that sealed our fate. Devon, who also wasn't a cat person, suggested that Sophie move into his studio apartment.

Now let me make one thing clear: I was nowhere close to marrying this guy. I had just gotten out of a relationship (and he was just getting out of a marriage), and I was still enjoying being somewhat single. But with no other options, I agreed it was best if Sophie moved in with him.

Looking back, I think Devon knew exactly what he was doing when he offered to take in Sophie. He'd figured out that if my cat and my boyfriend were living together, there was no way I would be able to stay away—and he was right. I decided to sleep over that first night in case Sophie needed me. I never left.

I also must admit that, for a non-cat-person, Devon was pretty damn cute with Sophie. He'd patiently sit and watch football as she kneaded and nuzzled his chest, his arms, or his beer can. And he figured out that if he rubbed Sophie's nose in just the right spot, she'd go into a Zenlike state complete with heavy purring and rolled-back eyes.

Within a year, Devon and I were looking for a one-bedroom apartment together. I'm not saying that we wouldn't have ended up together anyway, but that six-pound ball of affection definitely pushed us together much faster than we otherwise would have moved.

And so, for a while, life was good. We rented a pad in the city where Sophie was free to knead two heads of hair and stain the furniture with her eye gunk. (By this point, I'd figured out how to minimize the problem by giving her medications and regularly rubbing down her face with a wet paper towel, but it never completely went away.)

A year later, Devon and I got married and bought an apartment in New Jersey. Sophie was stoic throughout every change—she was just happy to have two loving humans all to herself.

Little did she realize there would soon be three. I don't blame

Sophie for disliking baby Jack in the beginning. After all, he did little more than cry and eat. And since I was breastfeeding, there was no space on my lap for Sophie. Still, she'd give it the old college try and attempt to climb over Jack as I was nursing him. When that didn't work, she'd sit on Devon's lap and meow in his face until he scratched her nose. She sought affection from anyone who visited our apartment. The minute any visitors would stop by, Sophie would jump on their laps, give them a quick swipe with her paw as if to say, "Forget about the baby, look at me!" then settle down and start kneading away.

Our family unit continued in much the same way until Jack was eighteen months old. That's when Jack decided he loved Sophie so much that the only way to show his affection was to sit on her. The worst part is that Sophie would take it—she wanted attention so much that she'd tolerate a twenty-eight-pound toddler flattening her into a pancake. Sophie was so delicate that I was convinced she'd be seriously injured in one of these "sitting attacks." But no matter how many times I told Jack no and pulled him off, then moved Sophie to higher ground, it would happen again. Things quickly spiraled downhill for the Sophster after we moved to a house in Connecticut. Despite lots of cash shelled out on tests and prescriptions, Sophie's eyes remained gunky. I'd resigned myself to a life of cleaning up brown stains, but Devon was starting to get fed up.

It wasn't long before Sophie's fate was sealed. To furnish our new place, we bought an area rug for our living room. We laid it down, admired it for a few minutes, and left the room. When we returned five minutes later, we were horrified: Sophie had decided that the weave on the rug was the single best thing she'd ever kneaded. It was nothing fancy, but we'd owned the rug less than half an hour and it was destroyed—covered with pulls and claw marks.

I'm sure you can see where this story is going.

"That's it! The cat is gone," Devon announced.

To top it off, I became pregnant again. At this point, even I had to admit that Sophie wasn't getting the affection and attention she deserved, and I knew it was only going to get worse after another baby appeared on the scene. But I'd always believed that once you take on the responsibility of a pet, it's yours for life. My parents had owned our dogs from the time they adopted them until they died of natural causes (which, in one case, was seventeen years later!). I didn't feel right just giving Sophie away. So I tried my best to lay a guilt trip on my parents and asked them to take her—just for a few years, until the kids were older, I said. After all, now that my dad was retired, they had plenty of time on their hands to focus on a cat with an almost manic need for love.

They weren't as enthused. "Well, a cat doesn't really fit with our lifestyle," my mom said. "And to be honest, I don't want my furniture covered in eye gunk."

A day later my mom left a message saying she had great news. I was hoping they'd changed their minds and decided to take Sophie. Instead, Mom informed me that she'd found her a home: A recently divorced woman she worked with was looking to adopt a cat. Her daughter was grown and she had the time and energy to focus on a love-starved pet.

At first, I said no. After all, Sophie was my first baby—I couldn't just give her away to some stranger. But after thinking about it, I realized that this was the best thing for both of us. Sophie needed tons of affection and wanted nothing more than to be held. I just couldn't give her what she needed. So I agreed—with one stipulation: Under no circumstances would Sophie ever be sent to a shelter. I would take her back no matter what—no questions asked—for the rest of Sophie's life. The woman agreed, and within two weeks Sophie moved into her new home.

The rest, I guess you could say, is history. My mom gives me occasional reports about Sophie, and they all go like this: The woman who adopted her loves her to death and refers to her as "my baby." Sophie sits by the door every night waiting for her to get home from work, then sits on her shoulders while they watch

TV, then sleeps on her pillow at night. Oh, and the eye gunk doesn't even seem to bother the woman that much (thank god!).

I must admit I miss Sophie. She was so loving and so cute (in an ugly sort of way) that it would be hard not to. But I think I did what was best for her. She's getting the love she so deserves and desires—and she no longer has to worry about getting squashed by an overzealous toddler.

The Neighborhood Watch Group

Judy Sutton Taylor

♡   I rang another doorbell of another neighbor I didn't
know, my fingers stinging in Chicago's early-April chill.
My mind was in overdrive: I hoped the person who answered
the door wouldn't think I was trying to sell something and slam
it shut. I hoped I wouldn't come across like a kook. I hoped I
wouldn't cry.

It had been a full week since Toby, my fourteen-pound
fluffball of a cat, had gone missing after climbing though a hole
in a window screen, and a sense of desperation was starting in.
Impossibly soft with a purr as loud as a car engine, Toby was
like a big, cashmere hot water bottle who curled into the curve
of my stomach every night. But he was also the kind of cat who
darted at any strange noise or sudden movement; friends who

had visited me dozens of times had never even seen him. So the excitement I'd felt the previous night when I spotted him around the corner in an alley disappeared as quickly as Toby did—he was just too scared and out of sorts to recognize me or the sound of my voice, and I lost track of him in seconds. I had spent the last seven days visiting shelters and wallpapering the neighborhood with Lost Cat fliers, and the last seven sleepless nights searching under porches and behind garbage cans. I was relieved to see that Toby seemed unhurt. But I was also losing hope that I'd ever get him home.

I was about to ring the bell again when the door opened. A middle-aged woman in a flight attendant uniform asked how she could help me. I explained about Toby, how I had seen him in the alleyway behind her back yard, and how I hoped she might let me set a trap in her yard that night to try and catch him. "I'm sorry," she said. "But I'm allergic to cats." She shut her door before I could say anything more.

I had been volunteering for years with animal shelters around the city: walking dogs, fostering animals who needed temporary homes, organizing fundraisers. I knew enough about cats to know that they didn't wander from place to place like dogs. Cats stay put, so Toby was probably still somewhere near that alley. I'd called in some favors and borrowed a few of the trap/cage hybrids the shelters used, hoping the strong scent of tuna in the still of the night would lure my always-hungry boy out of hiding and into one of these metal contraptions, a spring door snapping shut behind him. I figured that with a few traps securely placed in the back yards that faced the alley, he'd be safe while I made the rounds checking them. What I needed were a few neighbors— who, at that point, were mostly strangers—to allow me to go into and out of their yards throughout the night.

My husband and I had moved to our new house six months before, and I'd given birth to twins a couple of months after that. Unpacking and round-the-clock feedings took up my every waking minute; getting chummy with the neighbors hadn't been high on my priority list. Our pretty, shingled A-frame was in an older, less-than-trendy part of town, and the truth is that I was a little apprehensive about coming across as an obnoxious yuppie with my sidewalk-swallowing stroller and the super-size coffee that was perpetually glued to my palm to keep me functioning. I hadn't exactly gone out of my way to be neighborly, but no one had knocked on our door, either.

This is why people move to the suburbs, I remember thinking those first few months. *Everyone there has giant strollers, and people bring you Bundt cakes when you move in.* Needless to say, no one had come by with any cake for us.

But losing Toby was exposing me to a neighborhood I otherwise might never have gotten to know. Snippy flight attendants notwithstanding, walking the streets and back alleys at all times of the day and night reminded me why I loved living in the city.

The burly, tattooed guy with the long, gray ponytail who

Toby

owned the bar at the corner took a stack of my fliers, offering to pass them out to his regulars. "My cocker spaniel died three weeks ago," he told me. "They get to be like your kids, don't they?" The hippie lady across the street who homeschooled her three boys sent them out hunting for Toby every afternoon. (The white calico they brought me, excitedly anticipating their reward money, wound up becoming a part of our family, too. But that's another story.) The rottweiler-walking dude who I often saw in the park (and who I had always suspected was in a gang) stopped to tell me not to give up looking.

My toes were perpetually numb from the cold and I felt defeated, but I didn't give up. I was furious with myself for not noticing the window screen. What kind of mother was I going to be to my twins if I couldn't even keep my cat safe? All I wanted to do when I wrapped up my walks each afternoon was get home and lock myself in the bathroom so I could sob out of the baby sitter's earshot.

I set traps in the back yards of six gracious neighbors for the next two nights. The tuna lured a steady stream of possums that scared me as much as I scared them—but still no Toby. Then, late on the tenth night after Toby's disappearance, our phone rang. A woman who had seen one of my fliers had just pulled into her driveway from that alley around the corner. She'd seen Toby's collar tag reflect in her headlights, then watched him squeeze though a small opening to the cellar of an apartment building next door, she said.

While I stayed home with our sleeping babies, my husband ran over there. The building's super unlocked the cellar for him, and after two solid hours of careful, quiet coaxing, he was able to bring Toby home in a carrier. A vet checkup the next morning showed him to be dehydrated and seriously dirty, but in good overall condition. When we got home, the old Italian lady who had lived a few doors down from our house for the last forty-five years—the same one who'd wondered aloud if we thought we had moved to one of those "rich-people neighborhoods" when we hired a landscaper to spruce up our front yard—brought over manicotti to celebrate. Hey, who needs a Bundt, anyway?

Love Triangle

Erin Torneo

 Say what you want about single girls and cats, but a girl can learn a lot about love from a feline companion. Dog love is too easy. Cats, on the other hand, with all their complications, are the creatures that help prepare you for that tricky human love business.

I grew up surrounded by stray cats I would bring home (much to my father's increasing dismay). They had the run of the woods behind our house, returning at night to sleep in the garage, safe from coyotes and winter. With the cats came all the love offerings: baby bunnies and birds dropped off, half dead, on our doorstep. I took them as a direct challenge to my rescue abilities. One summer, we had several shoeboxes dotting the brick ledge of the fireplace, an infirmary of limp-necked animals that I nursed in vain. I had yet to learn the laws of nature and the laws of love, and that's where Hisashi buri came in.

I got her a few months before my college graduation. She was half Persian, half mutt—the love kitten of two friends' cats. I hadn't intended to get a cat, but when I saw her in my friend's apartment—those hazy blue eyes a contrast to her black, black fur in her still alien-proportioned little face, I somehow knew we belonged to each other. But I suppose she knew first. While my friend told stories about her recent trip to Asia, this fluffy little two-pounder marched in, hopped onto my lap, and mewed at me expectantly: *When are we going home?* And so home I took her, and gave her a proper name. Her uninspired litter name, "Blackie," didn't suit her, but Hisashi buri (the Japanese expression for "Long time, no see," my friend said), did—especially because that annoyed-sounding meow *(Where have you been?)* would become her trademark. She's a gorgeous animal, but when she opens that mouth I swear she's Fran Drescher.

Home was more of a roving concept back then. Where exactly I'd end up in the next fifteen to twenty years was uncertain, but I knew this cat would be with me. Hisashi buri—Sashi for short— was the sole constant in my peripatetic twenty-something life, which involved several starter careers, two cross-country moves, a year abroad, and three failed relationships.

Sashi was willful from day one. I attempted to train her to walk on a leash (hey, it worked on my pet rabbit!). We got as far as the front door of my apartment. In the hallway, she planted herself like a statue and refused to budge. She flashed me a look that distinctly said, *Not happening. Don't even try.* Some people would argue that's because cats aren't "smart" enough to be trained, but anyone with a cat knows the opposite is true: Most cats are *too* smart to submit. Here's how I know: I had given her a red collar with a red bell to accompany the leash, which promptly disappeared a day after our failed promenade. I couldn't find it anywhere in my apartment, and I was dumbfounded as to how she got it off, considering her lack of opposable thumbs. A week later, cleaning out her litter box, I unearthed the red collar. Not only had she removed it herself, but she had buried it in a strategic effort to prevent further humiliation. She had made her point.

I've often wished I could have her conviction, her absolute sense of self. It would have saved me from a lot of heartache. Cats aren't people-pleasers, the way girls are socialized to be. They are self-contained, and never reckless. They won't plunge into a relationship without careful consideration. Sashi is not desperate for affection, but if she loves you, you'll know it. You have to earn her love, and keep working for it. Thrust into a new situation, the first thing she does is secure her hiding spots and her escape routes—one tip I picked up after the demise of a particularly torturous relationship.

When that relationship ended (and like most painful processes, there were a few half breakups before the final

Sashi

cleaving), she instinctively seemed to know that there was a physical absence, a void. Sashi always made sure some part of her was touching me as I slept, whether it was the round pressure of her little spine against mine, or an outstretched paw placed on my arm. I was keenly aware of the stereotype of trading a cat for a man when I spooned her back, but I didn't care.

A few months later, Sashi was the lone witness to my brush with NYC crime. Someone got in through the unlocked roof of my Brooklyn apartment, and bashed in our front door with a shovel while my roommate was out and I was away on business. The door was metal, so it must have taken a long time (not to mention a lot of noise) to warp it enough to get in. My roommate called to tell me that among the missing items were a floor-model VCR, a $15 thrift store bike, some costume jewelry, and my cat. Sashi was MIA for three days until my roommate, thinking she heard phantom bells from the collar we'd forced on her, found her. She must have clawed a hole in the box spring under the mattress and gone into hiding. When I returned home, she took to patrolling the foot of my bed, which faced the hallway and the newly replaced front door. Whenever the vestibule door opened and she didn't recognize the footsteps coming up the stairs, she would growl.

I started dating Sascha—his similar-sounding name long a source of confusion for my mom—a few years later, and naturally he and the cat were rivals. She mostly hid when he came over, making an appearance as soon as he left. And then I started spending nights away, a grievance she protested by giving me the cold shoulder whenever I returned, suddenly demonstrating a pronounced preference for my roommate. If Sascha slept over, Sashi was relegated to the foot of the bed, a state of affairs she resented. Whenever he got up in the middle of the night to pee, she would claim his body-warmed spot in the bed next to me, sprawling out as large as her eight-pound frame would allow her to. But in addition to protecting her turf, I think she wanted to protect me. *Who was this guy? And why should she trust him?*

I had approached the relationship with Sascha with the same guardedness. This time, I was on high alert for the thieving kinds.

I secured my escape routes and hiding places. I was entirely self-contained and made the poor guy work for any ounce of affection. But month after month, I could not find a reason to continue my mistrust. Despite myself and in testament to Sascha's perseverance, our relationship blossomed.

But there was another hurdle: the love triangle between Sashi, Sascha, and me. Living in separate apartments kept the peace, more or less. But then Sascha and I decided to move in together.

She was the last thing I moved to his place, and she showed her protest by squawking loudly in the cab on the way over. When I let her out of the carrier into our new home, she skulked around with her belly low to the ground, pursuing the dark corners and meowing into the folds of the towels hanging on the rack in the bathroom, looking for a way out.

The following weekend I went away, leaving the two of them alone together. I had no idea what I'd find when I got back. But when I walked into the apartment, the first things I noticed were the toys: balls with bells inside, catnip-filled mice. I hadn't bought her toys since she was a baby. And then the two of them, sitting on the couch like old pals just waiting for me to drop by. She wasn't perched in his lap or anything—it was much too soon for that. But they occupied their respective ends of the couch with equal footing. It was a good start.

Cat Call

Suz Redfearn

I never fancied myself the type to get all gaga about a cat. Really stupid gaga. But sometimes hormones and other factors outside one's control force a person into ridiculously doting love affairs with pets. Usually it happens to childless females of baby-bearing age, like myself. If the classic arc is followed, things get worse with time, and before you know it, these women are signing their Christmas cards with little paw prints and buying pricey birthday presents for little Spot or Princess.

It used to strike me as loony, but not anymore. When an intense trans-species kinship threatens to occur, my advice is to throw common sense to the wind. Just go with it. I did.

My fall from grace began in 1995, not too long before I turned thirty. A simple phone call set it in motion.

"Okay, I've found a black-and-white cat for you," chirped the woman, a member of a pack of New Orleanians who took in strays. She'd been on the lookout for me since I saw her newspaper ad about a fresh batch of (all gray, it turned out) kittens. My deal, I told her, was this: I needed a black-and-white pet badly, having recently left a five-year relationship that had at its center a fabulously fun and jocular feline of *noir et blanc*. Unfortunately, my ex had acquired the cat a few weeks before we started dating, so when the end came, Fatty was his. I needed to replace him (Fatty, not the ex), and fast. A pattern was developing: the unforgettable two-tone border collie my family had when I was little; a perhaps unhealthy fixation on Sylvester the cat; and now this. Me minus a black-and-white pet was like a maritime man minus the sea. It was just wrong.

The animal lady agreed to put the word out on the street for me. That was months before; I was starting to think she was giving me the brush-off. But then one night, lying in bed, I had an aural vision. A message entered my head, almost like a telegram. It said, *You shall have a cat. He will come soon. And you will call him "Habbib."*

Habbib? I thought. *I don't know what it means, but all right.* And a few days later, the phone rang.

"He's over in a house by the river, on Tchoupitoulas Street," underground-network lady said. "You can go see him."

Lil, the tiniest little slip of an old lady hunched over and dressed in purple polyester, met me at the door of the rundown old shotgun-style house. A chorus of yaps and meows rose up behind her, and when she gave me the tour I saw that the entire house was filled with dogs and cats. No furniture or people—just animals and cages.

Most of her boarders were in sad shape, covered in mange or missing a leg or an eye. I felt pity, but I also bristled at the thought of the road pizza Lil was sure to try and get me to take home. I began strategizing. What excuse would I use not to adopt it once I saw it?

The last room on the tour would have been the front parlor if actual people had lived in the place. There, Lil pointed to a wire cage stacked on top of two or three others. "Meet Sylvester," she squeaked.

All I saw initially was his fluffy black-and-whiteness. *Score!* But when "Sylvester" turned to give me the full frontal, I was stunned. I had envisioned a normal cat, with a normal cat face. This one looked more like, well, Gizmo from the movie *Gremlins.* His face was flat—eyes, nose, and mouth all on the same plane. His eyes were massive, as were his paws. And thanks to the weird tricks genetics can play, he seemed to have a permanently disgruntled look. It was downright disturbing.

Nope, I said to myself. *Nope, not gonna do it.*

Lil opened the cage and Sylvester slunk out, eyes fixed on me as his body took its sweet time sauntering in my direction. I had to admit there was something intriguing about his attitude and the way he moved. He was so casual. So *Dean Martin.*

I plopped my butt on the room's one chair to watch him.

Habbib

Sylvester—his head had perfect Sylvester markings, but his body was the reverse, mostly white with the occasional black spot—jumped down off his cage and drifted toward me. But when he arrived, instead of lingering at my feet and looking blank or meowing for food, he knew what he had to do.

He took the bull by the horns, crawling right onto my lap, standing on my legs and looking deep into my eyes, holding the penetrating stare without blinking.

I melted like the wuss I was. Suddenly, he seemed flawless, quintessential. Up close, I saw the massive scope and soulfulness of his outsized amber and black eyes. There wasn't any disgruntlement there. His mouth may have been formed into a permanent frown, but this guy was all sweetness. And there was a sense of wisdom about him, too. And confident eccentricity.

And open-mindedness. *Jeez, I thought, how could all this be present in the eyes of a cat?*

Then it hit me: Obviously this was Habbib. Of course. With his facial structure, he had to be Persian, or at least part Persian, as in Middle Eastern, as in *Habbib*.

While the profound bonding process was underway, Lil jabbered away, telling me she had been the first person in Louisiana to spay and neuter animals without a license. In fact, she'd long ago removed Sylvester's manhood. Seems he'd come to her as the flotsam thrown overboard after a bad divorce. He was about a year old, she said. I was barely absorbing anything, other than the enormity of this cat's eyes. "I'll take him," I said.

After a rigorous interview process and a one-month waiting period, I was able to whisk the little Buddha home. Habbib needed a good scrubbing and a workup at the vet after all that time among the indigent. His ears were filled with mites and his skin was crawling with fleas. He emerged a beautiful cotton ball, one that meandered around in slow motion checking out my apartment.

Our early life together was, well, *interesting.* While I worked during the day, Habbib took to redecorating my pad by jumping up on shelves and sweeping them clean, covering my floor with broken vases and scattered books. Somehow I didn't mind. Miraculously, I also didn't mind that he was jumping up on my bed at 5:00 AM and purposefully waking me with a series of silent meows delivered directly into my ear. All I could hear was cat lips smacking, as Habbib had virtually no voice. *Maybe something's missing in his throat,* I thought.

That was the beginning of our ridiculous love fest. Now, six years later, my infatuation's so bad that I have to stop several times a day to stare at him. I can achieve a sort of high by doing so. When he gets up on the bed at night to sleep in the crook of my arm or near my head, I feel so flattered. And when he conks out on the floor on his back, I have to go and get my man, Marty, and show him Habbib's curly belly. Poor Marty.

Thankfully, Habbib digs me as much as I dig him. He spends about two-thirds of his day following me, angling to be as close as possible. Sometimes all I have to do is walk into a room and he starts purring. Lately he's taken to tapping me on the arm with his outsized paw when I'm doing something other than petting him. *That's enough typing, please,* this gesture says, or *I believe you're done reading now.* All of this, of course, does wonders for the self-esteem.

Not too long ago, I learned that in Arabic *habbib* means "darling" or "sweetie." I'm not surprised. Some pals from Morocco told us that when listening to radio stations in Saudi Arabia, one often hears singers croon, *"Habbeeeeeebi."* I'm not surprised at that either.

Habbib's got it going on. What validates me is that others are into him, too. At least two former coworkers who come over for parties have been reduced to puddles of goo around him. One woman announced in public that she wasn't going anywhere near any cat unless it looked like Habbib. Others ask if they can come over to visit with him, not me. Even my mom—not a cat person—is charmed. She requests cat pictures.

Like a dog, Habbib comes when called. His dislikes include sneezes, the vacuum cleaner, and being picked up. His likes include crows flying outside, strings whizzing by, grilled pork, and reclining on the adjustable kitty window ledge I got him for Christmas.

Of course, we've had to do some adjusting over the years. When Habbib stopped focusing on hygiene in 1998, mats began to form in his thick fur. Rather than sit on the floor and brush him for hours each night, I decided to start having him shaved like a schnauzer. Shaved bald, Habbib's body is a real disaster. He's swaybacked, and the loose skin of his gut just about drags on the floor. Plus, he's outrageously pink under all that fur. It's really hard to stop staring and giggling. It costs $40 a pop but it's worth it.

The first time I had it done, the groomer advised that I keep people from making fun of Habbib's new look for the first few days. "He'll be sensitive," she whispered. But hours later my pal

Mike came over and laughed hysterically the minute he saw him. Habbib didn't mind. He's just *that kind of dude*.

When Habbib and I moved from New Orleans to D.C., I continued shaving him, but I began to worry about the cold. He was an indoor cat, but still, there were drafts. Did he need an outfit in the winter? Perhaps some fleece? I went so far as to shop in the small-dog-ensemble section of my local Petco. The selection was appealing, but I couldn't go through with it. Not because it was a ludicrous notion, but because I was afraid that if left alone all day in a fleece jumpsuit, Habbib might accidentally get caught on some random hook and hang himself. I resolved to never shave him in winter.

Once in a while I lie around ruminating on what Habbib must have been like as a kitten. I regret that I wasn't there to see it. And what breed were his parents—both Persians? One Persian and one mutt? A mutt crossed with a Furby? When he blinks his huge eyes, he really does resemble a mechanical creature made for a movie set. There are never any cats that look quite like him in the cat books.

One time, I asked a vet what he thought Habbib was— meaning what breed. He scrutinized him from various angles, then held his hand up to obscure Habbib's face.

"When I do this and look only at his body, he looks like a rabbit," he said. He wasn't joking.

Our lives together haven't always been smooth, though. One day about three years ago he was sitting on the toilet lid, hanging out with me in the bathroom. When he grew bored and jumped down from the toilet, the impact of landing on the tile floor caused everything below his waist to suddenly go violently spasmodic. His legs were kicking and jutting and stamping wildly, and his tail flung back and forth. Thinking he'd dislocated a hip, I leapt out of the shower and tried to put it back into its joint. But nothing was out of place. He continued spazzing for another twenty seconds or so, then whatever seizure he was having ended. He looked at me quizzically, but there was no pain in his eyes.

A freak occurrence, I figured. An anomaly, I told myself. I moved on. A few days later, though, it happened again. Pretty soon, Habbib was contorting involuntarily several times a week, giving me a small coronary with each bout. *What was wrong with my Habbibi?*

I asked around. The consensus among cat owners was that it was either a brain tumor or a severe neurological problem. I feared a life without Habbib. I also feared the vet bills. How much would brain surgery cost? Two thousand dollars? Three thousand dollars? I began to prepare for grief ahead. I called my mom. She suggested that, if I chose surgery, I ship Habbib to Florida for his recovery. There, she would serve as his doting, full-time home health aide.

But all my agitation was for naught.

"It's just that he's too fat," the vet said when I took him in. "There's too much weight on his joints when he jumps down. Put him on a diet." I did, and within weeks, the fits stopped and Habbib went back to normal.

Besides that scare, and the occasional skin condition, things had been just fine in the health department—until recently. Habbib had taken to hanging out next to his water bowl with his chin soaking in it. I knew he had eccentric tastes, but this seemed a bit much. I called the vet. She said it sounded like the bizarre behavior that comes with old age. *But he's not even that old,* I thought. When I'd gotten him, little ol' Lil had told me he was one. Upon Habbib's first checkup, though, the vet had said, "Well, no, he seems to be about four." Either way, he was no more than . . . elevenish.

Within a few weeks, though, Habbib had started vomiting and pooping outside the litter box, leaving puddles of pudding everywhere. I got on the Internet one night to search for a diagnosis, and all signs pointed to—oh my god!—acute renal failure. Death was the next step, all the websites claimed.

I freaked. I ranted internally. I cursed the cat gods. *Cruel Fortuna, don't take my Habbib!* That night, I had trouble sleeping.

In the morning, I got out my new 35 mm camera and took sappy, maudlin close-ups of Habbib's face. I cried. Then I called the vet. She was all doom and gloom, just like the websites.

"He's crouching over the water bowl? Yep, sounds like dehydration from renal failure."

"But outside of the crapping and vomiting and crouching, he seems fine," I pleaded.

"Yep, that's what cats do. They mask their true feelings. You need to bring him into the ER right now."

I did, visions of loss clouding my head. After a long wait and much pregnant uncertainty, the vet came in and fiddled around with Habbib. The poor thing, he'd dropped two pounds—20 percent of his body weight; that's like twenty-four pounds for me!—but apparently his vitals were fine. They did blood work to test for renal and liver failure, and Habbib and I left with some kitty Kaopectate and rattled nerves. The next day, the blood work came back stellar, and Habbib's furious expulsions gradually faded. "Could have been a bug," the vet said.

What I'm going to do when Habbib *does* bite the dust, I have no idea. I can't even fathom it. Given the level of devastation I experienced over his latest crisis, I might lose it altogether when he gives up the cat ghost. Or maybe I'll start having babies and make the natural transition to treating this celebrated creature like the average house cat—one that had better get off the damned dining room table, one that will be out the door the minute he becomes more work than he's worth.

Then again, I highly doubt it.

Home Free

Susan T. Lennon

 I told my cat that we'd moved from our condo to a house so he could finally run free.

Little did he know our new yard was a fortress. Before we let him set one sleek black paw onto the grass, my husband, Donald, and I had barricaded it with a six-foot fence, put up netting to block access to the treetops, and stuffed rocks into the small spaces where the vinyl didn't quite meet the grass. Yep, we were feeling pretty smug. We figured that we'd mastered the art of worry-free outdoor-kitty companionship, giving Atticus what he wanted and outsmarting him at the same time.

Little did we know who we were messing with. Taking advantage of our complacency, Atticus must have been changing the channel from Animal Planet to Turner Classic Movies while we slept. I can just picture the little beast studying Steve McQueen, twirling his whiskers as he figured out how to foil us.

The late-spring air was laden with lilacs and freshly mown grass the evening Atticus carried out the Great Escape. We were lounging on the patio when I spotted a black blur streaking across the yard. Looking like a flying cartoon squirrel, Atticus defied gravity, landing on the latticed top beam. I sprinted after him, making smoochy noises in a lame attempt to disguise my true intent, and reached out to grab him. He flashed his emerald eyes, swished his tail, and jumped. To the dark side.

Barefoot, I tore back down the yard and through the front gate, stopping at the scrubby backside of the fence. Suddenly, a rasping yowl sliced through the silence, and although I could barely make him out in the dim light, relief washed over me as I realized he hadn't actually gone anywhere. Crouched atop a rock, his hair standing on end, tail as thick as a raccoon's, he shrieked like a child with a scraped knee. I bent down to reassure him, ignoring the depth of his distress, assuming that I could simply scoop him up and carry him home. He had other ideas. He hissed and spit and narrowed his eyes to slits.

"Come'ere, Atticus Catticus," I crooned as I bent over to grab him. He bit me. Hard. I dropped him as blood splattered the fence and ran down my arm.

Then I did what any cat mother would do—I snatched him back up and held on, even as he sank his teeth into my hand again, even as he screeched and writhed and scratched my arm. I hoisted him over the fence, where Donald, who'd run into the house for the Sherpa bag, captured him. Once inside, we tended to my multiple wounds as Atticus's electrified fur slowly returned to its usual smooth sheen.

He rubbed up against my leg, eyes beseeching, and that's when I realized that this kitty-boy, he of the hoarse meow, the hundred variations on *mrrrrrrr*, the proud panther who doled out his head-butts discriminately, was not the same cat who'd just attacked me. That cat, Atticus's outdoor alter ego, was some mythical monster whose empty eyes should have told me that he didn't—couldn't—"know" me out there. I was a predator to him, and he'd reacted accordingly. Nothing personal.

So, while I held no grudge, I did reevaluate my indoors-only-unless-supervised-in-the-yard policy. Over the course of the year since I'd rescued him, I'd tried every trick I knew to turn this former stray into a contented inside-cat—obviously unsuccessfully. It mystified me. Outside, he was edgy, skittish, dangerous; inside, he was macho, affectionate, calm. Yet he took every opportunity to run; he'd even pushed out a slightly loose screen and fled from the twelve-foot roof off the upstairs bedroom.

Now, even with a big, safe yard, he still pined for the thrill of pure freedom. If he truly wanted to be a road warrior, I guessed I had to honor his wishes—for real.

So that's how Atticus officially became an outside cat during the day. Every time I held the door open for him, I felt a pang

Atticus

of loss. I missed him. I missed his lap snuggles, our fake-mouse chase games—okay, full disclosure: I even missed cleaning his litter box!

When he came back every night, he was listless, guarded, and bedraggled. Still, like an addict, he kept seeking the buzz. His drug of choice? Someone else's grass under his feet, towering trees, the wind at his back, the unknown.

When we set off later that summer for a two-week vacation in Cape Cod, I feared that Atticus would be miserable: I didn't want to risk losing him in a strange place, so I planned to keep him inside the whole time. Little did I know that he would reveal his true nature.

The Cape house had floor-to-ceiling windows overlooking a salt marsh, and sliding glass doors that led to a wide deck. Breezes floated through the screens, the eelgrass swayed hypnotically, and the yard was flush with squirrels, chipmunks, and shorebirds. Fat lazy bees, butterflies, and hummingbirds frequented the hanging flower baskets, with the sounds of warblers and distant summer insects as a backdrop. After arriving, Atticus indulged in a luxurious stretch, plopped himself down in a patch of sun, and began to preen.

Over the next two weeks, Atticus bloomed. He groomed endlessly, returning his fur to its patent-leather shine. He rubbed our legs, gave us head-butts, *mrrrrrr*ed and purred and cuddled. He stalked the inside of the house, claiming it as his own. Not once did he try to escape.

We watched, not recognizing our cat. I realized then that I had read Atticus all wrong. He was just like a young teen—testing the margins, looking for adventure, pushing to get his way—but really hoping for love, security, and limits. Give kids too much freedom and they can't handle it. Here Atticus had been signaling to us all along that he was scared of the outdoors; his pining for it was a pretense.

And so he became an indoor-only cat—this time for real. Understanding his need for boundaries, and afraid to deprive him cold turkey, I bought him a two-story playpen—black wire, wood floor, two perches. This way, Atticus can experience the ecstasy of the outdoors yet still remain safely ensconced. He spends the rest of his time at home, content to yawn and curl up next to me on his window bed, right where he's belonged all along.

The Feline-Female Connection

Clea Simon

A black kitten, still in the roly-poly phase with a round, fuzzy body and a pointed tail, curls in the woman's hands, mewing in that high, beseeching tone young kittens have. It was a present, an adorable one at that, but still she drops the kitten in horror (it wobbles away unharmed). After all, she knows what such a gift means. For a single woman of a certain age, owning a cat signals the end of her viability as a sexual female.

Okay, so the movie *Three Coins in the Fountain* (which gives us the above scenario) might have been laughably square even when it was first released in 1954, and such rigid gender roles have gone the way of the mandatory girdle. But even more than fifty years later, the myth still resonates: You can have a cat, or you can have a sex life. Claws in, girls, that's the rule.

"Not another single woman with a cat!" I still recall the male office colleague's response the morning after a blind date with one of my (cat-owning) friends. But even as he disgusted me—she was too good for him, anyway!—I wasn't surprised. After all, it wasn't anything I hadn't ever heard before. Women with dogs may be outdoorsy, sporty, or fun. Substitute a feline, and we're either weird or sentimental or the kind of girly-girls who dot our *i*'s with hearts. Or we are feminists, man-haters, and thus of no use to our critics. (Lesbians seem to be immune to such bias, thank the goddess, though that doesn't help us hetero girls much.) Our feline friends aren't valued any more than we are. Socks was First Daughter Chelsea's pet and a White House resident until he was bumped out of first place in the presidential affections by Buddy, a chocolate Lab. Where did the displaced black-and-white end up? With Betty Currie, Bill's older, female secretary. A cat, after all, is not a proper pet for someone with power. But for better or worse, we've been lumped together: female and feline, throughout time.

The stereotype of the cat-loving spinster dates back for centuries. The original connection was basic: Cats, like women, are fertile creatures. After a pregnancy of about sixty-five days, most cats deliver several live kittens, and most are pregnant again within another two months. At the most primal level, such creatures became stand-ins for human fertility, both positively and negatively. Consider it homeopathic magic: Want an easy birth? Make sacrifices, or at least pay homage, to a cat.

There's a lot of supposition in this theory, but the archaeological evidence gives it weight. Take the famous Çatal Hüyük figurine, unearthed in Turkey, dating back about six thousand years. It's a crude but powerful statuette of a woman seated on a throne that's either carved with leopards or supported by the animals themselves. Wide-thighed, big-breasted, she appears to be giving birth. Her name lost to time, she's usually dubbed the "leopard goddess," but we have no way of knowing who she is, or why she was sculpted. Perhaps she is a goddess, delivering a divine litter. Possibly, she's an average woman, hoping to please the gods in charge of birth by holding on to two cats (or at least their images) as she bears down in labor.

Follow the same reasoning and it's easy to see why cats have long been identified with sexuality. Anyone who has ever heard the wails of a cat in heat or witnessed the males hissing and sparring to win her favors can understand why. To watch a female cat in heat, as she arches her back and displays her vulva, is to see desire in its most raw form. (Never mind for a moment that the male cat's penis is barbed, which one would think would remove the allure from the act itself.)

Add in the inherent sensuality of a cat, the soft fur, the lithe form, the warm figure eights a friendly feline will weave around your ankles, and the sex and sensibility connection becomes clear. Fur is sexy, so are cats, and we and our genitalia have been called "puss" or "pussy" since Elizabethan times.

But this is a good thing, right? I mean, the connection makes you think soft and pettable. Something that you'd like to curl up with. So where does the antagonism come from? Where the fear?

One reason for this fear is that cats are mysterious, and are often identified with magic and death-defying acts. For one thing, their flexible spines make them more agile than many other animals. A falling cat has a better shot than we would at getting her feet under her and landing safely, and to witness such a sight might convince a starry-eyed observer that the cat was immune from death. To add to their mystery, cats' excellent night vision allows them to see clearly, and therefore have freedom of movement, in the dark. It also allows them to scare you out of your wits when you least expect it.

Because of this mystery, and therefore because they're often misunderstood, cats, and symbols of cats, have over time come to symbolize magic. Of course, it wasn't always bad magic, the evil of black cats and the like. Long before the "witch cats" of Halloween, cats possessed good magic. But as the centuries passed, that magic was just too scary—and our cat goddesses all became nasty witches, their loyal, fertile sidekicks recast as "familiars." This slander happened all over the Western world: Hecate, an Egyptian midwife goddess who was symbolized by magical cats, became the Greek goddess of change and the crossroads—a neutral shift. But by early Roman times, she'd been downgraded to a witch-goddess, possibly one source for the medieval witch of Christianity. Freya, a Norse divinity who flew through the sky on a sleigh pulled by cats, was also turned into something bad, and eventually slandered as

Musetta

a thief, seducing and stealing gold. And the great cat goddess Bast? The goddess in charge of writing, papermaking, and brewing beer? Well, just look what happened to the Egyptian pharaohs, their Cleopatra reduced to the seductress behind Antony's downfall! The attitude carries over to female characters in the present, too. Want to see the cat-woman equivalent of our "evil" black cat? Witness Catwoman, Batman's equal but doomed to the dark side, to a life of crime and, ultimately, failure. At least she stirred things up while she was at it, just like the mischievous little balls of fur we know and love. In art, in history, we and our stand-ins, our cats, have paid.

How do we rescue Catwoman? Or at least reach out to the poor black kitten? Magic. We need to reclaim our power over our own image. We need to assert Catwoman's sensuality as a positive force. We need to defend our mystery as our own—sometimes positive, sometimes something darker—and be proud of our ambiguities and dual natures. We are feline as well as female, with all that implies. Here, kitty, kitty. It's time to change the world.

L.A. Gossip:
Tall Tales of a
Wild Cat in the City

Valerie Cabrera Krause

There is nothing I like more than hearing gossip. I don't even need to know the person being discussed. In fact, I like that my friends don't all interact with each other because then I get to hear the highlights of their friends' lives without anyone worrying about it getting back to them—and is it really gossip if you don't personally know the people in question?

A good storyteller is hard to come by, and most stories yield unsatisfying results. One standout exception is my friend Bernard. Bernard is *full* of stories. Bernard's stories are always true, and while he may exaggerate for dramatic effect, I also think that he is just one of those people to whom emotionally unstable people are drawn. What that says about me I am going to ignore for the purposes of this story.

Bernard's tales involve work scandals, rude waiters, the friend who is ignoring him, the ex-friend who called him a bloodsucking vampire—and then there's his shut-in friend, Faith. Faith hadn't ventured outside since she'd been attacked by a mountain lion, and instead took in smaller versions of the beast: cats.

I can't remember how I was introduced to the tales of Faith, but after four years of hearing the stories, I still have yet to actually meet her, which is fine by me and really for the best, since I have heard the most intimate details of her life.

I first heard about Faith when she was part of a couple; both of them had worked at the bookstore where I met Bernard. When he first discussed her with me, she worked in the accounting department of an entertainment company and was only mentioned in passing. Then her boyfriend broke up with her and the story really got good.

After the breakup, I received reports of Faith's weight gain. Significant weight gain fascinates me in a way that only a girl who has been on and off Weight Watchers for a ten-pound overage and lives in L.A. can appreciate. There is something forbidden about large weight gain in Los Angeles. Bernard waited for me to ask the right questions (he likes to build the suspense) before giving up the goods. And I complied: "Do you see her eating a lot?" "Does she exercise?" "Does she have to buy a whole new wardrobe?"

Valerie Cabrera Krause

He told me that she had been laid off from the accounting department and was now working from home. But Bernard knew that he hadn't answered all of my questions. He held some in reserve, which I appreciate in the same way I do a good movie trailer. "What about personal maintenance?" I asked. "Does she wear clean clothes?" Bernard completed the picture for me when he let out that she didn't even go out for haircuts and had hair "past her ass." My mental image complete, I thought that it couldn't get much worse—or, depending on how you looked at it, better.

As for her near-miss with the big cat, Bernard filled me in: Faith had been hiking in the Hollywood hills (L.A. hiking is sort of "hiking lite") when she'd come face-to-face with a mountain lion. How she got away has always been hazy, but this near-miss was supposedly why Faith stopped going into nature and, eventually, outside at all. Where some people would take the event as a don't-waste-a-minute-because-it-could-be-over-in-an-instant, life-affirming sign, Faith went the other way, choosing to stay inside her apartment whenever possible.

Bernard stopped hearing from her. She wouldn't make plans and seemed incredibly uncomfortable when he would pop over at her house to make sure she was still alive and well. Then, out of the blue, she called him. She had seen a feral cat in her dumpster and wanted to take him in. Bernard was glad to help her with the kitty rescue; he dropped what he was doing and went right over. It took a couple of nights to finally corner the cat—who, it seemed, had never lived in a home and was indeed feral. Considering his part done, Bernard left Faith and her new cat to bond.

Thinking that the kitty rescue was a sign of Faith's emergence

Heather

from an increasingly agoraphobic existence, he decided to pop over one evening in the middle of the week. He didn't see the kitty anywhere. Faith had already had two cats, both of whom were lounging on her couch. "Where's your new kitty?" Bernard asked. She said that it was too wild to mix with her other cats, so she was keeping it in her bathroom. Bernard was horrified, but he knew that letting her know would only cause her to re-excise him from her life, so he kept his mouth shut. On subsequent visits Bernard spent as much time as possible in the bathroom, trying to love Heather, the name Faith gave the cat, but Heather was not interested in affection and tried to get as far from him as possible.

Bernard didn't know what to do. Part of him felt like he should call animal welfare, but he just couldn't bring himself to do it. What would they do, anyway? Euthanize her? Would that be better?

To make matters worse, Bernard found himself on the outs with Faith. After seeing her drink an entire two-liter bottle of Dr. Pepper in one sitting, he'd said (in what he described as a light-hearted manner) that maybe she should switch to a less caloric beverage. He was just trying to be helpful, but at six foot three and barely 150 pounds, he shouldn't have been talking to any woman about calories.

Over the next few years, he would hear from Faith when she had a new plan for losing weight and getting back to a normal life. He listened (and, in turn, I listened) to tales of supplements, thyroid tests, diets based on blood type and myriad others—but as soon as she was off the wagon, he was off her list. Then Bernard's own cat died. Bernard loves cats and always has at least one in his care. He called Faith and broached the topic of adopting Heather. At first she refused, but Bernard was incredibly persistent; he kept asking every few months. Two months ago, Faith agreed. Every week after that, Bernard would tell me that this was the weekend he was bringing Heather home, and then every Monday I'd hear another lame reason why Faith couldn't do it that particular weekend.

A month after she'd initially agreed to it, Faith showed up at his house with the cat and a pair of scissors. She wanted a haircut. He cut her hair to just below her shoulders, and as he went to sleep that night he thought of the delicious symbolism: She'd released the cat from her prison, and in turn she had freed herself. And though he didn't tell me this part, I'm sure Bernard saw himself as the savior of both of them.

Last Bernard heard, Faith was back in her apartment. He hasn't spoken with her since the day she gave Heather to him. Heather has yet to adjust to Bernard's place, and he is considering finding her a new home. And I'm waiting for the next episode.

Saved by the Cat

Melinda J. Combs

 "Ohmygod, there's a cat in the road that's been hit by a car. Did you see it?"

"No. Are you sure it's a cat?" I figured it was a possum or a raccoon, since they often turn up dead on the highway.

"Yes, and its head was up. It looked so scared. I totally saw it," Jennie held her hand over her mouth, steering with her other hand.

"Well, let's turn around and get it," I said without hesitation.

"I'm glad I'm with you. I knew you'd agree," Jennie said, touching my shoulder.

Somehow, I've turned into the go-to animal person among my family and friends, probably because they know how much I adore creatures. As a child, I tried to save wounded birds, and as an adult, I save even the smallest of creatures: snails. When I see them scooting across the street, I pick them up and move them aside (of course, in the direction they were already heading in), so they don't get trampled. This can prove to be quite a task on a rainy day.

But although I don't hesitate to save the smallest creatures, I'm not really a cat person. Maybe because I was attacked by one a few years ago. One minute I was reaching down to pet a friend's cat, and the next thing I knew I heard hissing and felt claws scratching down my forehead, barely missing my right eye. The attack landed me at the doctor's office for scar treatment on my face (fortunately, the scar isn't noticeable anymore). Ever since then, I've been suspicious of felines and their moods (do you blame me?). Let's just say that I would, without hesitation, stop to save a dog, but I might—and that is a very *small* might—hesitate to save a cat. But because I was with Jennie, the mother of a stunning tortoiseshell calico (one of the very few cats I *do* like), I knew that we must stop. For everybody's sake.

So, we pulled over.

When we made this mutual decision to stop the car and help the cat, it suddenly pulled us together. The night hadn't started out that way: This was the first moment of closeness between us in well over a month. Returning to "us"—the way we always were—felt comforting. Admittedly, I longed for some distraction from the tension between us. Neither of us does well with conflict and our drive only proved how much we wanted to dance around our issues.

"So, are you as sick of Brangelina as I am?" I'd said in the car, looking out the window.

"Can't the entire planet just move on already? And who makes up these couples' names? What kind of a job is that?" she responded, eager for the distraction.

Of course, we avoided any topic about L. J. and my dating him—the source of our problems. She wanted L. J. to take me on a proper date; she didn't like how he pulled disappearing acts on me, only to reappear when I least expected it; it wasn't what, in her mind, I deserved. I had previously vented to her about L. J.'s worst qualities: He would barely take me out, but for a cup of soup at a local diner (after some prodding) and a movie. Our relationship mostly consisted of drinking some beers together at my place and rushing into the bedroom. Yet I saw qualities in him that I appreciated and needed at that time: intelligent conversation (he did have his MBA, after all), playful humor (he made me laugh so hard sometimes that my cheeks hurt), and undeniable chemistry. Jennie didn't understand what I was doing with him, though, and, at her earliest opportunity, told me to dump him. Her reaction made me feel judged and angry, because I just wanted to feel supported no matter what.

Thirty seconds after seeing the animal, Jennie parked the car and we sprinted onto the median to search for the cat. Dodging semis and SUVs—in the dark—looking for this little orange cat, we walked back and forth on the median and in the street, asking each other, "Are we in the right place?" "Where could it have gone?" At one point, we didn't notice a semi headed straight toward us; fortunately, the driver honked loudly. We had almost given up when we spotted a young girl across the street, riding her bike in circles, calling to the cat. Jennie and I then realized that the cat had darted away to hide in the bushes. Once again, we dodged cars while crossing the street.

Cat

The eleven-year-old was prepared to save this creature: She showed us the towels in her basket and the walkie-talkie she was using to report back to her parents. She pointed to where she had last seen the cat in the bushes. We decided to surround the bushes while our new friend covered the street so the cat wouldn't run back into traffic.

As we stood there, it was like we'd suddenly formed a united front: The distance between Jennie and I vanished. Our actions were about the greater good, so to speak, and not about *us*, not about going to dinner to hash out our problems.

"You got him?" I asked her, trying to peer through the bushes.

"Not yet, but he's heading this way. I can totally see him. He's so little, like a kitten," Jennie responded.

"Where is he now?" I asked.

"I got him. He's with me!" With a towel in her arms, Jennie caught the hurt cat. He was bleeding from his nose and mouth—certainly not a good sign. After saying a quick goodbye and thank-you to our angelic cat savior, we rushed to the car, which Jennie had unknowingly left running on the side of the road. We later laughed about how we'd been so focused on the cat that we didn't even worry about the car.

I drove to the after-hours emergency animal clinic while she cradled the animal. Driving her car felt awkward to me, like something I would have done before, but that now felt like a role I wasn't prepared to be in. When Jennie had asked that we meet to talk, I'd hesitated because I'm notoriously stubborn and have this habit (admittedly, a horrible habit that I'm currently trying to break) of shutting people out when I'm hurt, and not talking about it until I'm ready—which can sometimes be months later. I did that to Jennie. She didn't necessarily get the silent treatment, but I kept my distance. I was sulking.

"I'm so nervous," Jennie said. "My heart is pounding. The cat's breath is labored. He's struggling."

"Think calm thoughts. We don't want the cat to get more nervous. He can tell if you're upset. Try to slow your breath down, too," I said. I didn't know if my advice would help either of them: Jennie, obviously panicked about the cat, couldn't bear to lose this animal while it was in her arms, and we both knew that.

Once we arrived, we showed the front desk staff the bloody bundle in Jennie's arms. While they took him back for an exam, we filled out the paperwork in silence. We hovered around the check-in desk, asking and answering rapid-fire questions. It turned out that if no one claimed him, he would be placed in a shelter, but if he had to be euthanized (due to overcrowding), they would call us so that we could find him a home.

We read through the paperwork together. We discussed our options—the cat's options—and agreed on a plan of action. Our questions and concerns about the rescue highlighted the tension that had been brewing between us.

"What do you think is going to happen?"

"We can't let him die after we saved him."

"Do you think they're taking good care of him?"

"I hope it doesn't mean he's bleeding internally."

"Do you think they'll charge us? But we're being Good Samaritans. They have to save him. It's the right thing to do."

We agreed that if we needed to pay for his treatment out of our own pockets, we would.

This back-and-forth continued, giving us more common ground than we'd had in months, yet I didn't know how to respond any further for fear of saying something wrong. Our anger and disappointment in each other still echoed in the background, and even though I wanted to address the strain between us, I couldn't bring it up. I didn't know what to do or how to begin, really. So, we just spoke about the events of finding Cat, and our little cat savior, and how we wished we'd asked for her phone number to give her an update, and we worried that Cat might not survive. We even brainstormed potential adoptive parents.

When we were called into a waiting area to speak with the vet, we reviewed all the photos on the wall of doctors with their animals beside them.

"I hope *he's* our doctor," she said, nodding at a photo.

"Or what about him?" I pointed to an attractive man with his arm around an enormous yellow Lab.

When the vet (no one we had picked out, but handsome nonetheless) came out to discuss Cat, we listened tentatively: The animal showed signs of improvement; the bleeding had almost stopped; they still needed to run some tests; we would get the full diagnosis tomorrow. He commented on how nice we had been to save the cat.

After two hours at the hospital, we finally resumed our drive to dinner. We joked about the vet and how I should personally stop by for the medical report. Or maybe I should write him a personal note or an email. We laughed about all of my options, something she and I had often done with men in the past—until our impasse, that is.

Once we sat down to dinner, we needed to collect ourselves after the upheaval of the rescue. We talked about it over and over again—mostly because of our concern, but also to avoid our conflict.

But eventually I broke the ice.

"I appreciate you contacting me and wanting to talk since I can be so difficult," I said.

And from there, we sorted ourselves out, noting how stubborn, strong, and protective we each could be, while laughing at ourselves, as we always had. Somehow we kept returning to Cat, asking questions similar to the ones we'd asked in the vet's office, but the answers now had a more hopeful tone.

"Don't you think he's going to be okay?"

"I'm going to make an announcement in class about him. A student is bound to want him. How could anybody not want him? He's wonderful."

"He is a strong little creature. We saved a life tonight. We are so good."

And we were so good—finally. Even without saving our wounded feline friend, our friendship would surely have survived, but Cat forced us down that path much faster. I guess you could say that saving another creature gave Jennie and me the opportunity to save our friendship, too.

PS: I dumped L. J.

PSS: Cat found a home.

An Ode to the Murph Dawg

Susan Schulz Wuornos

Right after I graduated from college, a special guy entered my life. His name was Murphy, and he was a cat. Murphy was the runt of his litter, and he lived with his family in the bushes outside my sister Liz's condo. She and her husband, Ed, noticed that this one kitten always had to nurse last because all his brothers and sisters would go before him. Liz and Ed were worried the kitten might die, so they decided to rescue him and raise him as their pet. They named him Murphy and became proud, happy pet owners . . . for about thirty-six hours. That's because they'd chosen to ignore one small problem: Ed had asthma. They figured that since Murphy was just a kitten, maybe Ed would get used to the dander or something . . . you can probably see where this story is going. One night, a few days after they took Murphy in, Liz had to rush Ed to the hospital. His throat had closed up from an asthma attack, and he couldn't breathe. Needless to say, it was a scary moment for both of them and it opened their eyes about this cat.

So here's a reenactment of the next day, when Liz came over to my parents' house, where I was living at the time, since, as I said, I'd just graduated from college: "Sue? Can *[sob]* you *[sniffle]* take *[sob]* the *[sniffle]* cat *[sobbbbbbbbbbbbb]?*" She was crying so hard, *she* could hardly breathe! She was so upset that, even though I really didn't need (and couldn't afford) to be taking care of anything other than myself, I said yes. And the next morning? I woke up with a little ball of warm, cozy fur sitting on my chest, purring so loudly I could literally *feel* it. I was like, "Okay, okay, I can hear that you're happy. Now shut up!" But of course, at that moment, I knew it was all over—I was officially in love with Murphy.

And during the next eight years, he was the only "guy" who was consistently in my life and who treated me well (okay, he did attack me on more than one occasion, the little jerk! But I always forgave him; I couldn't help it). He'd watch me date all these losers—*ahem*, I mean, all these different guys—on my quest to find the One. And every time I'd come home either annoyed or heartbroken, there he was, waiting to snuggle with me.

Then came Saint Patrick's Day, 2001, the day I met Kevin. Unlike the time Murphy purred his way through my chest and into my heart, I didn't know in just one moment that I was in love with Kevin. I just thought he was cute and seemed nice. But over the next few months as I got to know him, again and again I thought, *Wow, he is a great guy. Down to earth. Likes to have fun. Has great friends, which means he can't be a jerk—otherwise those friends would have dropped him!* What I loved was that as much of a guy's guy as he was—football-watching, beer-drinking, Jimmy-Buffett-loving, boxers-on-the-floor-of-the-bathroom-leaving—he could also sit down with me and talk about stuff. He wasn't afraid to cry when he watched *Saving Private Ryan,* even though it was the fifteenth time he'd seen it. That's hard for a lot of guys to do. So that's why he was special. And that's why I knew I was lucky to have found him.

But there was one small problem with Kevin. Again, I bet you can guess where this is going. That's right: He was allergic to cats. So for the first two years we dated, Kevin never even set foot into my dander-infused apartment. And for those first two years I kept trying to persuade Kevin to get allergy shots. He refused, saying he'd tried them when he was younger and that they didn't work. That was probably the biggest "issue" of our early years together. I hoped he'd come around and decide to go for it—I didn't want to push it, because I felt like I was being a little rude trying to force him to get medicated just so he could come over and hang out with me and my cat. But then we talked about getting engaged. *How would it work out?*, I wondered. *How would Kevin and Murphy live together if Kevin couldn't* breathe *around*

Murphy

him? I didn't know. All I knew for sure was that no matter how much I'd come to love Kevin, there was still no way in holy hallowed Margaritaville that I was going to give up Murphy. Love me, love my cat, dude. That's all I had to say about it. And finally . . . after getting an apartment with two bathrooms—one for Murphy, one for Kev—and hardwood floors that could be easily de-cat-haired daily, Murphy did what Murphy was really, *really* good at doing. He purred his way right into *Kevin's* heart.

And we all lived happily ever after.

For about eight months.

Now brace yourself. You're gonna need an entire box of Kleenex to get from here to the end of this story. I can barely even write it; my eyes blur up with tears when I type the first letter of the first word of the first sentence. But here goes.

I mentioned earlier how Murphy was the runt of the litter. But under my years of TLC, of course, he'd grown into an adorable, king-size black-and-white cat. He'd earned various nicknames throughout the years: I called him Mr. Murph, my sister Liz called him Murphy-Durphy-Lurphy, my friend Samantha called him Murphonics. And Megan, an editor friend of mine, dubbed him Murphster. There was another Murphy Schulz (go figure!) at the vet we went to (Feline Health on the Upper East Side), so at the vet, he became known as East Side Murphy. And even Kevin had christened the cat with his own term of endearment: Murph Dawg.

Well, early in May 2004, two months before our wedding, I noticed Murphy wasn't eating as much. He was always a pretty good eater, which had led to his developing diabetes. It's common in New York City cats because they're well-fed and don't get enough exercise in our shoebox-size apartments. Anyway, even though Murphy had diabetes, we'd gotten his sugar levels stabilized—I'd give him his shots every day—and other than that, he was the same old cuddly cat who loved to drag his teddy bears around in the middle of the night as he made an odd, guttural meowing sound. So when I noticed he wasn't finishing his food, I thought something was wrong and brought him to the vet. They did some tests. I was at work when I got the call with the news that took weeks to sink in: Murphy had lung cancer. The vet said that they could do exploratory surgery to find out more, but usually, in these situations . . . well, it didn't look good. She told me to spend as much time as I could with Murphy, adding, "When it's time, you'll know."

Over the next few weeks, I was in denial. I kept trying to get him to eat. He still wouldn't take any of his food, but he'd eat his favorite tartar control treats (Murphy would always get compliments at the vet's because he had such healthy teeth. The secret was Pounce Tartar Control!). But after about a week or two, he stopped wanting those. I'd give him milk, which he enjoyed for a while. I'd watch his little pink tongue lap it up off a saucer. That lasted only another week, so then I tried pouring some of the juice from a can of tuna into his water bowl. At first he liked that, but soon it got to the point where he wouldn't even drink plain water. The weird thing was, even though he didn't seem to be ingesting any sort of nutrition whatsoever, he'd still jump up on the couch to sit on my lap, he'd use his scratching post, and he'd clean himself (hey, if he could lick his butt with his leg sticking straight up in the air, how sick could he be?). So even though it was obvious he was dropping weight, I just didn't think it was time. Every day, I'd come home from work, we'd hang out on the couch, and I'd sleep in the living room with him in his favorite spot.

Then early one Sunday morning in late June, I woke up and couldn't find him. I looked all over the apartment and finally spotted him. He was lying on Kevin's bathroom floor. He looked up at me, and seemed so sad. I petted him and talked to him, but he barely even responded. He was just so tired.

A few hours later he got sick, his now-skinny body just retching. And that's when I knew it was time. I called the vet and I don't even know how I said the words: "I think I need to come in and put my cat to sleep." I started to sob and couldn't stop. I could barely hear the woman at the vet's office tell me what to do. It was a beautiful, sunny day out, and here I was, having to face the worst moment of my life.

I put him into his cat carrier for the last time, and Kevin got a taxi. But when we got into the car, Murphy was so scared and I felt so horrible knowing what was about to happen that I had to take him out of the cage and hold him. He was so freaked out he peed all over me, and the sickly, sweet smell was something I'll never forget. Poor Murphy! Why had I put him through weeks of torture? Why had I been so selfish when he was suffering, his body betraying him with every passing day? I wondered if in trying to prolong his life I had only succeeded in putting him through more pain.

By the time we got to the vet, Murphy was so stressed he was wheezing. The vet brought us into the examining room and gave him a shot to make him comfortable. While he labored to breathe, Kevin and I petted him and talked to him and cried. Kevin, who a year before hadn't wanted to be in the same room with Murphy, was now in the room with him for his final minutes, feeling the same anguish I was. To see a six-foot-tall, broad-shouldered linebacker of a guy with tears streaming down his face over a cat isn't something you see every day. I loved Kevin so much in that moment because I knew he wasn't just there *for* me, he was right there *with* me.

It was so weird to know that in a few minutes Murphy was going to be gone forever. It was so strange to *know* that and to know our decision was creating that reality. That finality.

When the vet gave him the second and final shot, it took effect immediately. One moment Murph was doing that awful wheezing, then he was quiet. He looked like he was sleeping, like he could just wake up. I kept staring at his body, not quite believing that he wouldn't.

That was Sunday. The following Saturday, Kevin and I got married. I know it sounds corny, but I can't deny the meaning of the timing of it all. I truly believe Murphy was entrusting me to Kevin. Murphy had taken care of me for all of those single years of trial and error and heartbreak, and now he knew I'd found my true love. He knew I'd be safe even if he wasn't with me, waiting at home to greet me at the door.

People say to me, "Get another cat—it's the easiest way to get over the loss." But I don't want another cat. Even two years later, Murphy's still holding my heart for ransom from the place my sister Meg calls "the big scratching post in the sky." And from time to time I'll be in my apartment and I'll swear I see a little black-and-white body streak around the corner. Kevin says he sees it, too. It doesn't surprise me that Murph is now appearing as a cat ghost: He's just checking in on his work as a matchmaker, after all.

Cat Trap Fever

Margaret Littman

Natasha noticed before I did. Every night when I'd let my springer spaniel out into my back yard, she'd run to the concrete corner where I stored the grill. Instead of running and playing in the fragrant bushes, on the lawn, or even in the vegetable garden (her regular turf), she'd sit and sniff. And sniff.

Every day I'd look to see what all the sniffing was about. I never saw anything nestled behind the grill, although I did detect a slight unpleasant smell. Still, Natasha's fascination with the grill area continued: Seasons turned, leaves decomposed, but her beeline to the corner was steadfast.

It wasn't until it snowed one day that I realized what she had been after. While walking outside, I saw tiny paw prints in the snow. Not the tiny bird feet I had seen occasionally in previous winters. Not the deep, weighted prints Natasha made. These were . . . cat tracks.

Over the months even I, without a canine sense of smell, had come to admit that there was a problem. A few feral cats, if not a colony, had found refuge in my backyard urban oasis.

I had developed a reputation for rescuing and fostering dogs, some of whom had questionable hygiene issues and left their own marks on my garden (and in my house), but I had no idea what to do about these wild cats. All I knew was that I wanted them gone. My garden was not a litter box, and removing bird carcasses from the yard was not my idea of a good time. Not to mention, their late-night carousing was anything but quiet. Sleeping with the windows open subjected me to high-pitched hisses.

As much as I longed to get rid of them, though, I didn't want to be cruel: I didn't want to let my neighbor at them with a BB gun. Nor did I want to ask the city to set traps for them, because then they'd be euthanized, which seemed an excessive sentence for being homeless, loud, and messy.

Still, I stalled before approaching the one person who could help me—my friend Judy. Whereas I am strictly a dog person, Judy is an animal person. She has one of those sixth senses that allows her to find—and rescue—any living being. Dogs, cats, even pigeons have been saved by her one-woman animal kindness crusade. But I was afraid Judy would expect me to go to the same extreme measures she herself would go to for these cats. Donning armor and teaching them to trust people—inside her home—were not out of the realm of possibility for her, but they were for me. I had certain expectations of my pets. I didn't necessarily need them to jump up and greet me as I walked in the door, thus giving me a bloody nose, like Natasha once did. But I preferred a companion animal who didn't ignore me. Who at least *acted* like he or she needed me.

I vaguely knew about trap-neuter-release (TNR), a method used by everyone from animal rights advocates to some government agencies to control feral cat populations. I understood the N part of the equation. Neutering (and vaccinating) the cats had a bigger impact on controlling the wild cat population than euthanasia. It was the T and R I had problems with, as both promised to get me closer to the animals than I wished, and the R put them back in my yard, which was exactly where the problem had started in the first place. Neutering might prevent them from being able to procreate in my yard, but they'd still need to relieve themselves.

Eventually, though, I admitted that something had to be done, so I fessed up. Judy convinced me that trapping was the only answer that both was humane and promised to give me my garden back. As spring approached, she convinced me that there was some urgency—if we did it before the weather turned warm, we could get the cats before they had litters of kittens. We discussed releasing the neutered cats on a farm, or somewhere else where they wouldn't be a nuisance, but she had already called in

Salty

all the cat favors she could from kindly farmers. Still, she felt that releasing neutered cats where we caught them would reduce the number of cats, as well as their late-night fighting and mating noises, and their urge to mark their territory, which was what made my yard smell. She promised to help trap and take the cats (securely in the traps) to the vet, and even to help me release them after the surgery.

I emailed the local contact for Alley Cat Allies, one of the TNR promoters, to ask to borrow some traps. When I was out and about in dog-rescuing circles, people had often asked me if I knew her, so I figured she knew of me, too. She went by "Meg," which is my childhood nickname, and she lived just a block from me, so I was sure we'd click. She might even know these specific cats I was trying to trap.

Or not. Alley Cat Allies are the Leche League of animal

Margaret Littman

rescue: Part-time interest in the issue is not sufficient. I'm not sure if she sensed my disinterest in cats as companions, but despite my references from Judy and other feral cat rescuers, and my serious street cred as a dog rescuer, she would not loan me traps.

Judy, of course, had another secret supplier, and several nights later she showed up at my house with four traps, a thing that looked like a tuning fork, newspapers, blankets, towels, and can after can of things I don't normally keep in my house, like sardines, tuna, and wet cat food. She encouraged me to dribble and drip the smelly goods in lines up my driveway, enticing the cats into the traps. As I did this, stinking up my yard as much as the ferals had done on their own, and as my neighbors peeked from their windows, I worried that crazy-cat-lady behavior was contagious, even if you didn't have a cat to call your own.

On top of having four cats (one an ailing foster) and two dogs at home, Judy and her husband had newborn twins. She went home to live her life while I monitored the traps from inside my house. I watched my driveway's motion sensor light (which was tripped as often by ferals, rabbits, and raccoons as by people) and waited to see if I caught anything. It got late, and the traps were still empty. I wasn't sure if I was disappointed or relieved. Over the phone Judy and I agreed that we'd pack it in for the night, but when I went out to close the traps, one of them was thrashing around. My first emotion was relief that the mammoth tabby inside wasn't a possum or a raccoon. My second emotion was fear. I tried to toss a towel over the trap, a technique that is supposed to calm the animal. But that was about two feet closer than I wanted to be to this creature from the dark. (Also, it didn't work.) As it shook the cage I realized there was no way I was going to be brave enough to grab the short metal handle on the top exterior of the cage, load it into my car, and drive it to Judy's garage for safekeeping overnight. So I did one of the few things in my life of which I am ashamed. I made a mother of twin infants get out of bed at 11:00 PM, get in the car, and drive five minutes to my house to do a task because I was a big chicken.

In exchange, I agreed to pick up Salty (we had to name him in order to leave him at the shelter; he was gray, we were tired, he became Salty) after his surgery the next day, and drive back home, where Judy and I would release him together. (This, I learned, is where the tuning fork came in handy, to keep Salty away from our hands as we unlocked the trap.) I figured it would be a breeze; after all, an anesthesia-addled cat couldn't be all that scary.

In fact, he was still pretty damn scary. When I approached the vet's desk, Salty was still thrashing about in the metal trap, making it hard to carry to the car (despite still being covered by a "calming" towel). There was some blood on the newspaper under him, a remnant of his surgery, which contributed to his not-so-cuddly demeanor. And he was heavy. Salty was twelve pounds going on twenty, and he wasn't exactly enjoying the ride.

But as I got closer to him while loading the trap into the back of my station wagon, I got a quick all-God's-creatures glimpse of his vulnerability. This cat, who was the epitome of all the feline antisocial traits, actually did need me: to trap him, to vaccinate him, to keep him from procreating, and, most of all, to get him out of the trap as soon as possible.

So I obliged, and he ran from the trap and out of my yard. I never saw—or smelled or heard—him again. Salty was the beginning of my cat trap days. That night I set the traps again, and when I caught Pepa, the tiny black cat I suspected I'd catch the first night, I didn't need Judy to help me explain to my neighbors why this wasn't a crazy way to spend my evening. Nor did I need to rouse her from bed to touch the trap, either. But if I ever trap a collar-wearing house cat, Judy's getting a late-night call. Wild animals in my yard are one thing—domesticated cats as pets, that's another.

Country Cat
vs. City Cat

Amy Fishbein Brightfield

♡ We first saw her, crouched by the garage door, one night
as we pulled into the driveway. As Jeff and I got out
of the car and approached her, she ran back into the garage and
scampered up the stairs to the loft. A few seconds later, her pointy,
white-eared head peered around the corner and she gingerly made
her way back down the steps toward us. It was cold outside and
we weren't sure when she'd eaten last, so we thought we'd make
a friendly food offering. All we had was a half-eaten bagel with
cream cheese; as I leaned down to place it on the ground, she came
running up to me, licked my finger, and immediately devoured it.

We had just bought the house in the Catskills as a country
getaway; this weekend, we were there to figure out what
renovations it needed. Jeff had seen the cat before when he was

walking around the property with Rich, the previous owner. "You want a cat?" Rich had asked casually. Of course we told him no, we lived in the city, and besides, we already had a cat, Moomoo.

But on this chilly November afternoon it looked like the owner had left the cat behind for us anyway. We called Rich to tell him his cat was here. "Oh, if Kitty doesn't come back in a few days, I'll come get her," he said. A few days? But it was bitter cold outside! We couldn't just leave her alone at the house. "Oh, she'll be fine. We never let her inside. All of her nine years, she's stayed out in the garage." The garage? With the dirt floor and no heat? Maybe it was because we lived in New York City, where people treat their pets like royalty, but we just couldn't believe that this cat with long, luxurious white, brown, and black fur could be left to live outside.

Miss Kitty, as we started to call her, quickly proved to have doglike qualities: She followed us around the rest of the day, both inside and outside the house. Because we didn't have heat yet, Jeff and I slept with our coats on that night, and Miss Kitty slept right next to us.

We bought food and a heated water bowl and left the house that weekend worried about what would happen to Miss K. While Rich had assured us that she would find her way to his house (three miles away) if she needed to, a painter who had come to work on our house disagreed. "Cats get more attached to places than people," he said. "She's lived here her whole life. This is her home. She's not going to Rich's place."

The next weekend we drove up and Miss K quickly ran out of the garage, meowing to greet us. Clearly, Rich wasn't coming back for her—it looked like a cat was part of our country house deal. So Jeff installed two cat doors—one in the garage door and one in a side door of the house—and we put out boxes of hay in the garage loft so she'd have a warm place to stay.

We wanted to keep Miss K; we didn't want to give her to someone in the country because we worried they would just keep her outside as a farm cat to control the mice population. But we had a problem: There was no way we could bring her back to the city. We just had a small apartment, and of course there was Moomoo to consider. Moomoo would probably be okay with another cat, but we were more concerned about Miss K. After defending her turf from strange animals all her life, Miss Kitty would never be able to coexist in a small NYC apartment with another feline. Plus, Miss Kitty was a true country cat, hunting mice in the fields and woods, sleeping in the bushes that lined the house, and, most importantly, spending her late mornings and afternoons sunning herself on the side porch.

The temporary solution: Jennifer, a pet sitter who we found

by placing an ad in the local paper, the *Towne Crier*. Jennifer came by twice a week to feed Miss K and give her the attention she deserved.

Miss K lived on her own in the country for two years. On Friday nights we'd pull into the driveway and her head would appear in the cat door, her yellow eyes glowing in the glare of the

Miss Kitty

headlights. She'd wait until we got out of the car and then she'd hop out and run toward us, meowing in greeting. Then she'd escort us to the front door and immediately jump up on the couch, waiting for us to sit down so she could lick our hands and faces.

Throughout the weekend, Jeff would work in the yard, planting trees and flowers, and Miss K would be his right-hand cat. Sometimes she'd disappear for a few hours and we'd find her just sitting on a log in the woods across the street, contemplating life. To Jeff, she was the perfect girl: pretty, loving, and loyal. She was tough enough to defend her turf yet sweet enough to nuzzle her head under your chin.

But as much as we liked our weekend ritual, every Sunday night it seemed to get harder and harder to leave her. Jeff was especially upset about it, and I think part of it was that he didn't want to leave the country and return to the city, either. When we left, Miss K would usually be sitting on the back porch, but late one snowy afternoon, we saw her little head in the upstairs bedroom window, watching us as we pulled out of the driveway. We drove away in silence.

During the week, we'd worry endlessly about her. Would it be too cold? Would she get caught in a rainstorm? Would another animal make its way into her cat door and eat her food or, worse, hurt her? Jennifer sent us email updates on the days she visited, and we wouldn't be able to sleep without them.

Then one year later, Moomoo died suddenly of a heart attack. The apartment felt empty without her. We didn't want to be disrespectful of Moomoo, but one of the first thoughts that entered our heads was to bring Miss Kitty to the city. This seemed to be the perfect solution—no more pulling up to the house wondering whether Miss K would be there. But Jeff was still torn. He didn't want to deprive her of a peaceful country life full of lazy afternoons and twilight mouse hunts. Animals are very attached to their owners, I told him, so I'm sure she'd rather be with us all of the time than left alone in the country. Plus, now she'd have the best of both worlds: being in the city during the week and visiting the country on the weekends.

"But remember how she found her way back to the house

after Rich moved? She seems pretty attached to the country. Let's wait until the weather gets colder so she can enjoy the rest of the summer there," Jeff said. We also worried that all the horns honking, the sirens blaring, and the 5:00 AM *bleep bleep bleep* of the garbage truck would make her a neurotic New Yorker. We didn't want her to end up on kitty Prozac!

One October afternoon, though, we decided to go for it. As we packed the car, Miss K settled into her usual early-evening nap spot on the edge of our bed. I scooped her up in my arms, walked down the stairs, and climbed into the car; she meowed quietly but gave little resistance. For most of the car ride she sat on my lap.

Miss Kitty immediately took to city life. She carved out her favorite spots in our apartment: the radiator in front of the windows in the second bedroom in the mornings, a slice of the wood floor warmed by the midafternoon sun, and the end of our bed at night. Every morning just before 6:00 AM, she would quietly sit next to Jeff's head and paw his face. As soon as his alarm went off, she'd meow wildly, jump off the bed, and follow Jeff around as he got dressed for work. Miss K seemed like her happy self, except for one thing: her appetite. Anytime we, or anyone, went into the kitchen, she would scamper ahead and sit in front of her food bowls, staring at them intently. When we opened the refrigerator, she would squeeze her fluffy self in front of us, peering in at the bottom shelf. While we ate dinner she would perch at our feet, patiently waiting for any scraps to drop.

"She's depressed and is turning to food," Jeff said. "It's all she has to look forward to now that she's not in the country." Keep in mind, this is the same guy who didn't show this much concern for my well-being when there were four pints of half-eaten Edy's French Silk ice cream in the freezer.

"Give me a break. Cats don't get depressed and turn to food like humans do!" I responded. Don't get me wrong: I wanted Miss K to be a happy cat, too, but I felt that Jeff's concern for her was getting a little ridiculous. If he obsessed this much over a cat's emotions (that we weren't even sure she was capable of experiencing!), how would he ever survive having kids? Needless to say, he insisted on taking her to the country whenever we went. But the car rides back and forth proved to be less than relaxing. During bumpy spots in the road she would meow loudly and sometimes breathe with her mouth open—which, we learned, is like hyperventilating for cats. "It's okay, girl," Jeff would say. "We're almost through the bumps." At stoplights or in traffic he would reach back and pet her head. "Is her mouth open?" he would constantly ask. As cars whizzed by, Miss K would stare intently out the window, her head bobbing and ears twitching. So

Jeff devised an elaborate system to calm her down: We covered the backseat windows with towels.

Once in the country, she would immediately go back to her old ways, walking the property alongside Jeff as he planted trees and disappearing into the fields to bring us back little half-eaten brown mice. But at thirteen, Miss Kitty was getting older, and we worried about her ability to defend herself against other cats and even coyotes.

Fast-forward many meowing and open-mouth-breathing car rides later, throw in a fussy new baby, and we decided to leave Miss Kitty in the city, much to Jeff's dismay. "She spent her young, active years in the country," I said to him. "It's better for her to be in the apartment in her old age. She's safer there."

Last weekend, the car ride back from the country to the city took us three hours—and the baby cried for about half of it. When we opened the door to our apartment, there was Miss K, meowing to greet us. She followed Jeff to our bedroom and immediately jumped onto his lap and licked his face as he lay down on the bed. I braced myself, thinking Jeff would be upset that she'd been cooped up all weekend in the apartment by herself. Instead, he looked at me, smiled, and said, "It looks like Miss K is having a nice retirement in the city."

True Confessions:
I Was a Reluctant Cat Owner

Lisa Guernsey

I'm a recent convert to the whole cat thing.

Growing up, the closest I got to a cat was at the home of my dad's colleague. I liked it well enough, but then my eyelids swelled shut. It wasn't a bad case of the sniffles, like you see in sitcoms, when the adorable kids smuggle in a homeless kitten. It was a full-fledged, eye-closing extravaganza. I was the prizefighter on the wrong end of the fight. The evening—and my experience with felines—was abruptly cut short.

After that, I tended to keep my distance. Most of the cats I did get to know (however remotely) were affiliated with various boyfriends.

There was the baby tabby in Dundee, Scotland. It liked to play on the stairs, which was endearing and which I could participate in halfheartedly as long as my eyes were a safe distance away. I also used to meow at it, upon which the kitty would look at me quizzically, as if to say, "Are you talking to me?" Or maybe it just found my American accent confusing.

Years later, there was the fellow graduate student in the Bronx. He had a plush gray cat named Calliope. I liked the boy, seriously distrusted the cat. Calliope had a way of making it perfectly clear that all laps should remain unfilled only as long as the cat deigned it. Objections would not be brooked.

We all got along fairly well, until the boy went away for a few days. You see, I was not only the girlfriend, but the girl next door, too. Would I take Calliope? Okay, I said grudgingly, accepting my duty like a martyr.

Disaster! The cat trotted after me wherever I went. Nights were a purgatory. Calliope wanted to be in the bed with me and would not take no for an answer. (This, I had previously determined, was verboten; I still lived in fear of the next prizefight.) The kitty scratched at the door and cried nonstop. I put my pillow over my head and pretended not to hear. It was the howling that pushed me over the edge. In the battle of wills, I came up second. But what did I expect? It's a stacked deck when you're up against a nocturnal. (By the way, I found it beautifully ironic that one of the reasons this boy and I first broke up was because I was too "high maintenance.")

At about the same time, my family was, to my horror, getting in on the act. My sisters, both younger and still living at home, needed something furry and helpless to tend to. They ended up with the runt of a litter and a shy semiferal. Neither made much of an impression on me during visits, other than the asthma attacks, of course.

Then along came Callie. My sister Anne was living with me for the summer, and somehow—not to be understood in hindsight—she persuaded me that getting a cat would be a good thing to do. Callie was a pound kitty. She was a tough Bronx girl and had already been at the city shelter for three days, so we knew it was getting down to the wire for her.

A few days later, Anne brought Cal home after work and set her loose in our quasi-mousy Brooklyn abode. Emerging from the shower a few minutes later, my sister found Callie, dignified but indignant, waiting for her, a sticky mousetrap clinging to her front paw.

With a cat in the house, I relaxed a little about the mouse situation. For years, my landlord had been supremely casual about the problem. When I would go downstairs to complain, he would laugh and make jokes about "visits from Mickey." After Callie's arrival, I was pleased to realize how much less of a workout my peripheral vision was getting.

She also possessed, to my great amazement, a quirky personality. I'd thought all cats were graceful, acrobatic creatures; Callie could be, well, *ungainly*. After every misstep, she'd groom herself—a gesture we couldn't help but read as self-consciousness. The most easygoing of cats in Brooklyn—she would go limp in your arms if you picked her up—she turned into a holy terror at

Lucy

my parents' house, chasing the other cats and tracking down poor Stanzy by the sound of her snores (she'd sought refuge under a sofa). The summer ended. Anne and Callie went back to college. In the Brooklyn apartment, it was just me and the mice.

The following summer, Anne moved back in after graduation, seeking a job in the city. I found myself almost more excited by the prospect of Callie's return.

Shortly after, the idea of getting another cat began to circulate. Callie was "lonely," and another cat would keep her company while Anne and I were at work. Our new girl was another pound adoptee. I think she and I knew right away that we were meant to be a pair. She was terrified of Callie and spent most of the first evening behind the TV. Only in the middle of the night did she come out and plop down next to me. As my incredibly fuzzy vision picked up the movement of a little white blob from TV to chair to me, I decided upon a name: I would call her Lucy.

Lucy amazed us with her absurd fetching talents, and her ability to skid long distances. She and Callie eventually became civil to one another, and would chase each other around the apartment (which was quite something to hear from outside the front door). We learned how adhesive of any sort held a strange allure and that the smell of bleach would send Lucy into a rapture.

Anne eventually got fed up with the city and moved away, taking Callie with her. It was hard splitting up the two kitties, but there was no question that Lucy would be staying in Brooklyn with me.

My lifestyle would have to change. It had been easy to make plans in the evening when there were two kitties and a sister on the crew. But now only one person was around to take care of and amuse Lucy; I didn't like to spend the night away from her. It created a definite shift in my relationship with the boy in my life: Nick became much more of a frequent overnight visitor, which was inconvenient for him.

Then one morning at the diner, he had a stunner: He wanted us to move in together. Not what I was expecting, but we had been together for a few years, and I agreed with him. But did he realize that Lucy was part of the bargain?

Yes.

These days, I'm still Lucy's primary food and cuddle provider, while Nick is comfortable being the tireless playmate (though I've also noticed the food bowl has a way of magically refilling when I forget). But it's hard not to take it personally that she gets the first greeting of the evening when he comes home from work. That's okay—it's a small price to pay for domestic bliss.

Little Black Cat

Sarah Shey

The worst week of my life as a mother was spent waiting for Little Black Cat to return. Every morning at breakfast I speculated about her homecoming with my eighteen-month-old son. "Today, Henry," I said. "I know it." At bedtime every night, I realized I had been proven wrong. My son began to gaze at me, his hazel eyes hard, conveying for the first time since his birth that he could no longer trust his mother. He went about his mornings and afternoons a lifeless figure, drained of his usual vigor. I had never before realized how integral Little Black Cat was to our family. We had, in an instant, become lopsided.

To distract Henry from the loss of Little Black Cat, I had bought not replacements but cousins. Lots of little black cousins. First there was Carmine, who was named after our postman for no other reason than we liked Carmine (and his first name). The cat's luminous lime green eyes made his skinniness all the more alarming. Next there came Jelly Cat, a plump, bearlike animal who had an almost-too-long tail and looked like an overfed royal who desired nothing more than to spend the entire day snoozing on a divan. Then there was Oatmeal, who resembled a fluffier version of Little Black Cat—he had fashionable white markings daubed just so on his paws, face, ears, and tail. I trusted that after a period of bereavement, my son would be able to toddle onward—with a fresh cat in tow.

The plan seemed to work. Henry began to dote on Oatmeal. It helped, I think, that he was named after my parents' farm cat, whose impeccably licked body emanated long, frosted hair, a befitting hairstyle for the cross-eyed and often disagreeable empress she was. Oatmeal stepped in as my son's escort. Henry was once again soothed by something of his choosing.

The doorbell buzzed. It was six o'clock in the evening.

A bundled deliveryman appeared at our front door. I signed for a cardboard box. It felt cold. QUEBEC was stamped on it. My stomach flip-flopped. Could this be the day I had stopped mentioning Little Black Cat to my son because I had also begun to lose hope?

With my apartment keys, I sliced open the tape and tipped

over the box. Out tumbled Little Black Cat, who had been tenderized, so to speak, after months of Henry handling. Her paw pads were no longer white, her whiskers were no longer there, her tummy fur was no longer pristine, and her green eyes were no longer smooth. She was cold with a frozen face—that part of her body was always in some state of condensation—but otherwise in tolerable shape. Henry bit the place where her nose used to be.

Henry had first taken a liking to Little Black Cat (also known as LBC) when he was ten months old. For several weeks, he and I had been reading *Maisy Drives the Bus*. Maisy, a snow white mouse with beige ears and paws, was created by Lucy Cousins, a writer based in Hampshire, England. She devoted a series to Maisy and her entourage, which included a milk-lapping Little Black Cat, who, admirably, was always just herself.

The title page shows a smiling all-black cat, with six whiskers framing a peach nose. Maisy, in a green uniform, drives a green bus and picks up her five friends at five bus stops. The story ends when Maisy reaches over to wake Little Black Cat, who has succumbed to the motion of the bus. "Oops! Wake up, Little Black Cat," the narrator says. "This is the last stop."

"Mew, mew," I added. Henry looked at me. It was the look of love.

In the many Maisy books we accumulated, Henry sought out Little Black Cat, who finds herself in all sorts of scenarios: sitting on a tree branch, sipping milk on a farm, and acting as Maisy's sous chef. The Maisy books became, for a time, our favorites.

Little
Black Cat

I bought LBC as an afterthought. I had gone into a toy store to pick up interlocking cars from Sweden. But when I spied the cat, manufactured in China, I wondered how Henry would respond to it. He took one look and bit it. How did he already know the way of the cat world? The cat landed in the pile of the other toy animals—a wooden cow, a musical camel, a professorial panda. I had no idea if Henry was going to become one of those children dependent on a particular toy—but I had read up on the concept. In *What to Expect: The Toddler Years*, the authors write, "Though a toddler can't always take her parents along as she explores her world, she isn't quite ready to go it alone. A transitional object . . . provides a perfect, portable source of reassurance." A local toy store owner called these objects "irreplaceable and invested with magical powers." Adults prize such items, too: Holding a cocktail or a purse makes a soiree of strangers less nerve-racking.

Before long, Little Black Cat was plucked from obscurity. She began to have a favorite color (green). She began to be deposited in unexpected places: laundry baskets, shopping bags, cupboards, drawers, and eventually, the potty chair. Henry began to require her for naptime, calling for her by name: "Mew-mew, Mew-mew." And as if adopting cats' silent ways, Henry often maneuvered around the apartment on his tiptoes. Little Black Cat's nose was never the same.

I didn't mind Henry's devotion to a black cat. Although black cats have historically been associated with witchcraft and sorcery, and since World War I have been the symbol of anarchists, so many black cats populated my parents' farm in Iowa it was almost bad luck *not* to cross them. And, thanks to LBC's vanishing, our apartment now hosted a litter of them.

Due to LBC's cult status, she accompanied us on all our trips—or was it the other way around? She had been to Saint Martin, Saint Barthélemy, and Bermuda; Minneapolis, Miami, and Maryland; and my parents' farm, where she was pushed into the original Oatmeal's face, who leapt away from the guest who reeked of milk mustaches. LBC was, by far, the most indispensable object in our carry-on luggage—more so than diapers, crackers, or milk.

It was on just such a trip that Little Black Cat got left behind. One February, we traveled to Beaupre in Canada, a thirty-minute drive from Quebec City. Henry was too little to ski down Mont-Sainte-Anne or attend the *école du ski* or dogsled in the woods, and too young to find the cheek-stinging weather invigorating, so my husband and I took turns dragging him around the hotel in his sled while he clutched Little Black Cat. Sledding conditions were ideal: The hallways were treeless, the wind nonexistent, and the elevators uninhabited. When we weren't tobogganing, Henry enjoyed putting LBC "away." He put LBC in the microwave. He put LBC in the television cabinet. He put LBC in the blanket box. And the blanket box was the one place I failed to check when we left our room.

When we landed in Newark, my gut hinted—and my carry-on confirmed—we had forgotten to pack LBC.

I called the hotel on my cell phone. "We lost a little black cat—a *doudou*," I said. I had learned the French word for *lovey* from friends.

"Cat," I said.

"Cat," I said again. "No, not bag, *cat*."

"Does anyone know how to say cat in French?"

"*Chat*," someone hollered from the back of the airplane. Yes, that was right.

"*Chat*," I said. "*Oui. Chat. Chat. Negro chat. Chat negro.*" I looked across the aisle for affirmation. "Oh, *chat noir.*"

When we arrived home from the airport, Little Black Cat-less, we called the hotel again and learned they had found our *petit chat noir* in the room. (Good thing I remembered to tip housekeeping.) We gave them my husband's account number for an overnight delivery and expected to see the cat the next day, Sunday.

"Little Black Cat will be here soon," I told Henry. "When you wake up." Henry spent the night alone.

No cat showed up the next day. I rang the hotel.

"No deliveries on Sunday," I was told. Enter Carmine. Henry tossed him aside.

On Monday, still no cat. "The account number you gave us didn't go through," I was told. "Not enough numbers."

I called my husband at work, and indeed he had left out the last digit. "How could you?" I asked. I then relayed the missing number to the hotel. Enter Jelly Cat. Henry tossed him aside.

More days passed. No cat. Enter Oatmeal. Henry tossed him aside, only to later change his mind, as if, at last, he was reconciling himself to the unthinkable; Oatmeal was scooped up and squeezed.

In one of his many childcare books, Dr. Spock writes that if the transitional object gets lost, "the child will be in real despair," but he fails to mention the parents' agony. Each day I woke up with a cavity in my stomach and fell asleep with that cavity. I noticed how my son looked at me, how he studied the deliverymen bringing packages deficient of his cat. This was an inevitable lesson in the realities of life outside the womb (the first being the birth itself).

Seven days. Seven naps. Seven bedtimes. While other friends were selling software or defending an insurance company in court or tending to patients, I was preoccupied with the off-kilter shift in our family—the life extracted out of our household as if with a syringe. It was as if Oatmeal, the farm cat, had never returned from a midnight mouse-hunting expedition: The pangs of loss were that real. I felt silly, at times, over how much I desired Little Black Cat to return. I could not take my son's eyes much longer. I could not handle thinking that something so cherished was lost to us. Then LBC embarked from Quebec on an airplane, pit-stopped in Indianapolis, landed at the Newark airport, and was trucked to Brooklyn. Then the doorbell rang.

"Mew-mew, Mew-mew," said Henry, and he cradled his cat, who was as smelly as she was cold. I was happy because Henry was finally happy. I snapped a photo of the homecoming. Our home was righted, animated once more, buoyed by Little Black Cat's return. And the thing that struck me: It was the inverse of the fairy tale. Instead of a stuffed animal being brought to life by being loved so much, the opposite had happened. Our family didn't make LBC real; it was the other way around.

Planet Catnip:
My Life with an Alien Cat

Leah A. Zeldes

♡ For years, I've suspected that my cat, Max, is an alien. I don't know what planet he beamed down from, but he's definitely Out There.

For one thing, he likes to follow us around the house, watching intently, as if he's taking mental notes on all our doings to report to someone later. I work at home, so his favorite observation spot during the day is my desk. When he's not staring unnervingly at my computer screen while I type, he's sitting on my papers—he has a sixth sense of just which one I need at any time, and that suddenly becomes his favorite resting spot.

But anyone could argue that those are "normal" cat traits. The biggest hint I have that Max is not from this world is his abnormal reaction to catnip. Most cats, when exposed to this herb, become excited, euphorically sniffing, rolling around, shaking their heads, and rubbing against things. Even lions and tigers have this catnip response. Not Max.

Now, it's true that between 15 and 35 percent of cats don't react to catnip at all, and this is perfectly normal. The receptor for catnip—a physiological sensor to nepetalactone, a primary ingredient—is genetic. Because the ecstatic catnip response is somehow sexual—nepetalactone resembles a chemical found in the urine of female cats—very young and very old cats don't respond, either.

But Max loves catnip. He just doesn't respond the right way. Despite having a very poor sense of smell for a cat, another point for otherworldliness (and a condition our family called "nose-deafness" until we learned the proper name is *anosmia*), Max can detect catnip at a great distance. This is, in fact, normal—a cat's receptor for the nepetalactone molecule is located not in its nose, but in its vomeronasal organ, an anatomical structure above its palate. This organ also senses such olfactory signals as pheromones produced by other animals.

Cats can respond to catnip in concentrations as small as one part per billion. The thing is, though, the response is triggered by inhalation. Ingestion isn't supposed to do anything. Most cats chew on catnip only to release its volatile aromas.

Max, on the other hand, thinks it's gourmet food. His yowling, begging response when I take out the catnip canister is exactly the same as his reaction to a freshly opened can of tuna, and he gulps it down with the same relish as he would dried anchovies.

It's as if someone told him, "This is something that Earth cats like," without telling him how to respond to it. He certainly doesn't have the classic catnip response.

People don't have the catnip response, either. While a 1969 study in the *Journal of the American Medical Association* described slight psychoactive effects in people who smoked catnip, that study also mislabeled a picture of a marijuana plant as catnip. For humans, catnip is primarily a tea plant; its leaves and flowers can also be used sparingly in salads and as a garnish. Medicinally, catnip tea is said to relieve insomnia, flatulence, diarrhea, cough, nervousness, and headaches, and in large doses to act as an emetic. It also increases perspiration and menstrual flow, and is said to reduce swelling.

Catnip is also thought to discourage rodents, especially rats, but whether this is through its own characteristics or because it attracts felines, I can't say.

A hardy, perennial member of the Labiatae, or mint, family, catnip, *Nepeta cataria,* grows up to three feet high and about fifteen inches wide. It has coarse, heart-shaped, fuzzy gray green leaves, square stems, and a rather scraggly habit. Its small, tubular pinkish flowers bloom from July to September. Several catnip relatives, notably *Nepeta faassenii,* are more attractive border plants, but they don't have the same effect on cats. Certain other plants do elicit the catnip response, though: These include Tatarian honeysuckle, *Lonicera tatarica;* silver vine, *Actinidia polygama,* which is used

Max

to tranquilize lions and tigers; and valerian, *Valeriana officinalis.* I haven't tried any of those on Max.

Most growers recommend starting catnip directly from seed, since setting out transplants puts enough scent in the air to attract passing cats, who are apt to destroy the new plants before they can get established. ("If you set it, the cats will eat it / If you sow it, the cats don't know it," as the old rhyme goes.)

I didn't actually plant any catnip in my garden. It just appeared in our new yard right after Max got out one night and disappeared for three days—the longest time ever. Normally, he only tries to go outside in the spring. That's the time, we theorize, when he reports to his alien masters.

We were never able to trace where he went on his three-day sabbatical, though we searched the neighborhood frantically, fearing he wouldn't find his way back to our new house. Then, on the third morning, he was just there.

Soon afterward, the catnip sprouted. Now it spreads with no help, self-seeding around the yard.

Catnip is most fragrant and flowers best when grown in full sun, but in my yard it does just fine in light to medium shade. It prefers even moisture, but tolerates dry conditions once it's growing well. As with most aromatic herbs, drought will concentrate the essential oils, making the fragrance stronger.

I pick fresh catnip for Max whenever I happen to notice it, but harvest a main supply when it's in full bloom. I dry it in an airy place he can't reach by hanging bunches enclosed in perforated paper bags. I strip the leaves from the stalks before giving it to him, so he doesn't injure himself on hard stems.

Now that he's getting old—Max will be twenty this spring, as earth years are reckoned—he's gotten picky about what he eats, complaining bitterly about most of my offerings, but catnip remains his favorite treat.

He's also gotten wilier about escaping the house and tries more often. One day, he'll get out and return to whatever star-begotten place that sent him to us, and all that will be left to remember him by will be those catnip plants. It will be a sad day for his Earth-bound family.

Our Relationship
Went to the Cats

Kristen Kemp

My ex and I adopted seven animals during the seven and a half years we were together. Five of them were cats. While the stereotype is that single women suffer from addictions of the feline persuasion, my need for fur was most severe while mired in this relationship. After all, the craving for a soft, purring pet is really about one's need for attention, appreciation, and affection.

My ex (I'll just call him Shit-Smack, S. S.—his real initials—for short) was not particularly into attention, appreciation, or affection.

S. S. did not particularly like cats.

He wasn't into psychics, either, especially not psychics who channeled cats, but I get ahead of myself.

The story of our relationship, told in terms of our cats, goes like this: We adopted our first feline after two months together. This black-and-white kitten was much cheaper than a diamond ring, and he became the first sign of our commitment to each other. I was twenty-one; S. S. was twenty-four, and the cat, named Thurman Munson, was six weeks old. The hiss and poop between us—S. S. and I, not gentle Thurman—flew. I didn't see then that a creative, quirky, city-loving cat lover (me) probably would never get along with a serious, conformist, outdoors-obsessed frat boy (S. S.). He was cute, though—S. S., I mean, though Thurman was a looker, too. Eventually, I had to keep Thurman outside because he peed all over the house. Little did I realize that rabid dogs would eat him (poor Thurman!).

After Thurman's funeral, I begged S. S. to let me adopt another cat. Right before Christmas, we wound up in Borough Park, Brooklyn, at one of those classic cat lady houses. We adopted a Jewish cat named Yonah Schimmel whom we converted to atheism and named Catfish. He was into playing fetch with rubber bands, eating roaches, and climbing plants and Christmas trees. S. S. tolerated that fat furball in our apartments in Hoboken and Jersey City, and then in our house in Saratoga Springs, New York. S. S. wasn't into Catfish, but at least he didn't spend evenings with the cat downing six beers like he did when he was with me.

Catfish needed a friend—I said Catfish, not me—so I adopted a retarded orange cat and named her Wookie. No one liked Wookie. She hid under the staircase, under the bed, in the bathroom washstand, in between towels in the closet. I wouldn't see her for six days after S. S. had the guys over for football and cards. Around this time, I met two very cute, feral kittens in our neighborhood. The guy across the street said if they didn't get rescued, they'd "be kittencicles by November." It took me three days to catch those warm, fuzzy mammals with only a milk crate, a stick, some string, and several cans of tuna. S. S. put an ad in the paper, trying to give them away. I didn't return the calls.

The black kitten, a sweet girl, was named Bea after S. S.'s grandmother, a woman I adored. The yellow one was named Berzerk, inspired not by the cat's behavior, but by the state of our relationship. At this point, S. S. was not only into six beers a night and card games. He was also visiting OTB (Offtrack Betting) regularly, and a guy with no teeth started bringing over clear Baggies full of weed. I wanted to leave, but I loved the four cats— even mentally challenged Wookie—and our white dog.

I had choke-collared myself into an unhealthy relationship. The final paw was when he didn't come home on Christmas night. I was twenty-eight by then, and I finally realized that city cat (me) and country mouse (him) had no chance. It didn't matter

how handsome and brooding and tanned country mouse was.
I arranged for Catfish and Wookie to move in with S. S.'s sister.
The white dog would relocate to my mom's. Bea and Berzerk were
coming with me, to New York City. I had already lined up an
apartment on Sixty-Third Street.

As I packed my things, Berzerk went missing. S. S. and I had a

Hello

last hurrah posting LOST flyers around
town and driving around in his truck,
whistling, "Here, kitty, kitty." The cat
never returned. Bea and I left.

I was sad, but not alone. Because
of the painful memories, I renamed
my furry, obese, tuxedoed girl with
white paws. I called her Hello because

I thought it was funny when my friends said, "That's such a weird
name. Oh, wait a second. I get it." She and I slept together at night;
she let me hold her like a stuffed animal. I wouldn't date any guy
more than once if he didn't fuss over her, at least a little.

I was writer girl in the city, lost but blissful. One evening,
in an attempt to be creative and quirky, I attended a press party
for a new American Eagle fragrance. The party employed palm
and aura readers, and also a frizzy-blond-haired psychic named
Barbara. With things so uncertain in my newly single life, I was

drawn to palms and auras and to her. She spent five minutes with other creative and quirky types, but she spent twenty with me.

"He was a jerk," she said. She sat in a very unladylike way, her black tennis shoes planted on the ground. "His name was Shit-Smack." She not only got that right, but she also knew that my recently deceased grandmother was called Ruth. She correctly told me that the guy I'd been sleeping with was a no-good, alcoholic photographer. She even knew exactly how many books I had completed. At the end of our session, she leaned forward, feet touching my pointy heels, and added, "You're going to meet someone very tall, blond, from overseas. Oh, and did you recently lose a cat? A yellow one with a weird name?" I said yes, I had lost Berzerk. "Berzerk was hit by a car, and Ruth is up in heaven petting him."

I called S. S. and told him all of this, as I tended to call him when there was no healthy reason to do so. "That's psycho," he said, laughing. I could picture him telling the story to his football/card/OTB buddies. I vowed not to call him anymore, not even to see if he'd heard anything about Catfish and Wookie.

A few months after that, I met a six-foot-five Swedish man. Now, two years later, we are married; we are both city cats, definitely. We recently added two mammals to our family—our tiny twin daughters. We also have a cat that he loves. Her name is Hello.

You Can't Change
a Tiger's Stripes

Tracy Teare

First things first: I'm not a cat person. My experience with these creatures is largely limited to an occasional stroke for the skittish cats at the barn where I spent years mooning over ponies as a kid, and childhood visits to my cousins' house, where an anxious black cat called Fletcher and a feisty oversized tiger called Zinnobia ruled the roost. One of my sisters lobbied hard for a cat once, but after a cousin's visit in which Zinnobia streaked through our screen porch and fled up a tall pine, where only the town fire crew could reach her, my dad wouldn't hear of it.

Not that it matters whether you're a cat person or not. Most felines could care less what we humans think. They decide on their own terms if you're worthy company or better off ignored.

At least, that was the case with the cat that adopted my family when I was twelve.

It all began like this: One mellow spring afternoon, a white, orange, and brown calico cat showed up on our backyard patio out of the blue. She put on a show of meowing and rubbing against every leg she could find, leaving traces of her winter coat on

Tiger

our overalls. The cat looked healthy, but seemed starved for attention. We suspected she belonged to our neighbors, whose dark, mysterious house was separated from ours by thick woods and what at the time seemed like a sizable hill (at least from my twelve-year-old perspective). My two sisters and I—who as kids cottoned to four-legged, furry creatures like ticks to a deer—were thrilled by her visit. (Back then, our only pet was a painfully shy rabbit who lived in an outdoor hutch and hated to be touched, much less held or fussed over.) When the cat showed up again the next afternoon, and then the next, we figured she was unwanted next door and maybe even unfed. Soon she was a regular in our back yard. We named her Tiger, and she acknowledged our attention with the occasional dead mouse on the back step.

Not wise to the ways of cats, we fell hard. We begged our mother to let us feed her, and soon she was sneaking home small bags of Meow Mix and cans of Fancy Feast, all of which we concealed from my dad. Tiger ate everything with a gusto that we read as confirmation of our suspicions: She was hungry, she needed us, and it was our duty to take care of her.

Summer became fall, and the weather turned cool, so of course we worried that Tiger, abandoned outdoors, was chilly. After school, we snuck her into the house, careful to keep her down in the basement playroom, where our parents were less likely to see her. She didn't stay overnight—too risky!—but she certainly felt right at home. She watched us from her perch on the basement stairs, twitching her tail while we made up shows to the tunes from *Free to Be . . . You and Me.* She chowed down Meow Mix while we munched our graham crackers. She put up with our carrying and holding and petting. She even let us dress her up in an old baby bonnet and gown and push her around in our doll stroller (now *that's* something our rabbit wouldn't do!).

Then, just as suddenly as the visits began, they stopped. No more patio visits or limp chipmunks. No more enginelike purring. No more Tiger. Of course we were worried, and it seems crazy now, but we didn't dare call our neighbors to find out if

Tiger was all right. The neighbors had "big kids," and we were shy and stayed on our own turf.

Years later in high school, we were chatting with some neighborhood kids at the bus stop (including next-door-neighbor Mariah, who had seemed so intimidating to us when we were younger but turned out to be harmless and kind). A dainty black cat slipped by our group, which got us talking about Tiger. That's when Mariah told us Tiger was, in fact, really called Pebble. What's more, turns out another family down the road had had their own little romance with Tiger/Pebble. For a minute, my sister and I felt stung. Jilted by our own Tiger, after all those devoted hours of petting and purring and snacking and wheeling in the baby stroller.

But in the end, we just had to laugh, wondering who else Tiger had snowed. For all we knew, she had duped most of the street and had every other house lavishing her with attention and slipping her a little kibble on the side. Even now it makes me suspicious of cats. Are they *all* this sneaky? Are they in cahoots with each other? Kind of makes you wonder, what else are they pulling off? All I know is, when my neighbor's red tabby, Baxter, slinks over and turns on the purr, I'm not rushing out for Meow Mix anytime soon.

Kittens Think of
Murder All Day
Michele Mortimer

It is a Monday night. Around nine. My boyfriend and
I have just finished dinner, a salad that summer made
sweet with strawberries, and though it has been a long day for
both of us, we are not so cynical as to bodily reject a good dose
of blood sugar. We feel energized. We get giddy. The Mets are
playing the Phillies, and winning; they keep winning this season,
putting all circles of hell on red alert for a pandemic chill.

Hugo and Silas, our kittens, not yet six months old, are
following Tim around the living room; he strings a neon rainbow
teaser along the sideboards and up around the furniture, and
they scurry, they pounce, they attack, they do flips that would
have names were this platform diving or floor gymnastics. Hugo
gets wild in the eyes quick. He pants, his tongue flicks. That he

doesn't actually foam in the mouth is almost a letdown. Silas drops back at regular intervals, keeping low to the floor, not so much conceding leadership but asserting that subtle dominance that comes with keeping your fucking cool. He preserves his energy. He jumps strategically.

The neon rainbow cat teaser knows exactly who is in charge. Silas is the brains of this kitty operation. If they were a gunslinging duo of bandits, Hugo would hoot and howl and fire gleeful rounds into the sky, but Silas would do the dirty work, shooting direct to the heart or the back of the head.

I am enjoying a glass of wine. It is my second. It is a Monday, and on a Monday, one needs to drink, and when you have kittens, one needs to drink fast, because if there is liquid in a round container, be it glasses or the toilet, the kittens will shove their little faces in and quench thirsts they seemingly stole from large, parched, overworked packhorses.

The night is good and it is only the beginning.

I take my wine to the bathroom, resting it next to the soap, and begin readying myself to go out. We have tickets to see a band at the Bowery Ballroom—Dirty Pretty Things, imported from England, of the catchy rock tradition, born of another band, the Libertines, that withered after the lead singer shot up enough junk to justify breaking into a flat not his own and thieving as he liked. The flat was that of his guitarist. Also, his best friend. They disbanded. The guitarist then formed this new band, with mates who presumably refrain from helping themselves to his cherished belongings. Though far from passionate about this band, we like enough of their record to check them out live, to stand in a crowd of hipsters, pretending that we're not hipsters ourselves, for a few hours and a few beers and conversation shouted above the din. It is what we do, go to shows, and if too much time passes between shows, we experience low-grade headaches and acute irritability.

I attempt to salvage the mascara job done almost fourteen hours earlier and make a mess of it, smudging black in spots of my eyes that could do without. Hugo wanders into the bathroom, hops to the toilet seat, and decides the flusher needs a good spit clean. Silas is soon to follow and spreads out on the bathmat, likely plotting the plunder of ancient cuneiform texts or working equations to prove string theory a load of crap. They abandon individual pursuits and come together to conquer, without mercy, my eyelash curler. In the doorway, Tim stops to assess the scene— two kittens batting around a small medieval torture device—and is torn between thinking this cute or just one more slip down the slope of kitten discipline, when the phone rings.

I answer, in feigned breathlessness, hoping to impress upon

the caller that a rush is in progress. While we are not due to leave for another hour, that hour has no room for a conversation of any substance, and because the call has come to the landline, it is most certainly one with substance, and not of the snappy variety that typically flows through the cell. It is Carrie, whom I still call my best friend though we are lucky to talk once a month and when we

Silas & Hugo

do I hang up the telephone bewildered, a little dazed, much like when passing the corner where the good used record shop has always been, and still ought to be, were it not for this yoga studio that insists on being there instead. In my mind, this record shop still exists.

Carrie was my college roommate, a vegetarian, a feminist, an environmentalist, causes she took delight in promoting, particularly when it annoyed her audience. She had a fraternal twin, a beloved dog, a pair of overalls worth borrowing, and a free spirit that welcomed jugs of cheap wine, cigarettes, extended crying jags, tarot readings, eighties music, and whatever other whimsy of mine that cluttered our room. After twenty-some years spent in the state of New York, she moved to Alabama for graduate school; there, she fell in love, got married, and, by rituals she has not made verbally known, became Southern. Insolvency kept me from her wedding, from standing up as bridesmaid, and thus I have never been to Birmingham, Alabama, nor have I visited her since in Tulsa, Oklahoma, but these have been homes to her, and for that I am careful not to apply the easy stereotypes that come in the day when states are boiled down to red and blue.

Chad is her husband, and, like the territory to which he belongs, is also unknown to me. He has crossed the Mason-Dixon Line on a few occasions, so I'm told, but until documentation arrives confirming these dates, I remain suspicious that he and I are not able to find a mutual coordinate upon the Northern grid. I trust he is a worthy husband but he has a dear friend of mine regularly tailgating college football games. And smoking meats. When she told me this she abbreviated: "We've been smoking a lot." I thought weed. I thought hand-carved mahogany pipe. I did not think barbecue grill. I did not think pork ribs.

In a drawl that may have regional flavor but just smacks of Down South to me, Carrie interrupts my vivid and lengthy depiction of being almost out the door. She says this will just take a minute. In the interest of science, it takes less than a minute, even with a suspenseful pause, to tell someone you are pregnant. I think I say "Congrats!" and wish I had drawn out the word to its proper length. Firstly, saying "Congrats" makes me sound like something is lodged in my throat, as if my disposition is so dour, abdominal thrusts are needed to expel good cheer. Secondly, I need a moment. Another moment will prevent me from saying "That's wonderful!" with the enthusiasm I apply to, say, hearing about foliage. Foliage, people, is best experienced. I say this because autumn is fast approaching and it will be tempting, I know, to talk about that drive upstate, those many shades of orange. But I say "Congrats!" and I say "That's wonderful!" and I continue to speak, despite incontrovertible evidence for going mute, blathering, "Oh my god, I have to tell you, I'm so glad to hear this, after the week I've had, well, it's a long story, but my baby cousin, she's engaged, and I'm all ambivalent about it, but this, this is really great news, news that feels right, you know, and I'm so glad for you, really, I couldn't be happier." There are so many things wrong with this sentence—if one could even call it a sentence—I fear putting it on paper will incite a formal inquiry as to my ability to vote, use public transport, wield cellular devices, possess currency, and walk the streets sans helmet.

I am up at two, persistent bites at the straps of my tank top, Hugo on the left, Silas on the right. I jolt upright and both boobs pop out of my top. The kittens freeze in saucy poses, heads tilted just so, as if we have just capped off a *Benny Hill* skit. I am up again at four, hairs being plucked from my scalp, one after the other, and my yelps must grow loud because Tim awakens; he gathers both kittens in one hand and shuts them outside the bedroom door with regal gestures that should only be applied if your hands are gloved and your doors are French. I am up again at five thirty, hearing cries over the air-conditioning buzz. Silas cries once in a great while, as if his existential crisis has come to a head, but Hugo cries like a baby—constantly—and one can assume any baby would cry just the same if banished to hardwood flooring.

I slip out of the bedroom and begin the day. While the kittens tumble about, I take my coffee to the computer and decide to use this early start to catch up on work, defaulting instead to email. I write to my friend Jean, subject line: Knocked Up in Tulsa. Jean is also a friend from college. She lives here in the city and we have always shared an easy camaraderie. I finish my note and then just before sending the email I realize I have already told her the news. I left a message on her voice mail last night. I am unsure of the content, tone, or length of this message and hate myself for a good five minutes that my memory cannot withstand four drinks, and then hate myself for another five minutes that there is no taking this message back. I would like Jean to be the sort of friend upon whom I can comfortably deposit drunken, extempore ramblings,

but our friendship is measured into regular portions, happy hours
or brunches or park picnics or parties at which we condense
the progress and interests of our lives into summarized recaps.
Frivolous things are packaged in emails.

All of my friendships, in fact, are like this, lacking a
genuinely spontaneous element: no *What are you up to right now,*
no *Come on over and hang out,* no *Calling just because.* Whether it
is the condition of adulthood, wherein schedules are burdened
to the point that advance planning is required for even a quick
coffee; or the nature of city living, in which seeing friends often
requires an hour subway ride there and another hour back again;
or simply a personal defect that keeps my friends at this distance;
or a combination of any of the above, it is chronically troublesome.
A recent study has found that people today have fewer people to
confide in than they did twenty years ago. Twenty-five percent of
the polled group cannot name even one. Work is blamed, media
is blamed, and thinking about this study, I can almost hear the
strains of "Eleanor Rigby," those damn violins, that damn church
where a wedding has been.

I delete all that I have written to Jean, and draft something new:

Apologies for my drunken dialing last night. The baby
news is hardly surprising. Yet, on a Monday night,

I was on my second glass of wine, getting ready to
go back out to see a show that wasn't even starting
until eleven, and when your best friend from college
interrupts this carousing to announce she's pregnant,
it sort of seems like the universe clearing its throat,
raising an eyebrow, and asking, Um, is there a reason
you've deferred on leaping into the marriage/children
continuum? Is perhaps your development, oh, I don't
know, arrested in some way? And I'm sort of like, Hey,
universe, you know what, I've been with someone for
ten years, how come nobody goes all apeshit for that?
My kittens are no longer shoving their noses into my
asscrack when I sit on the toilet. Is this nothing to you?
Clearly I have my issues but there's this sense of being
second-class to those wedded and popping them out.
Or maybe sensing this is my issue. Whatever. Carrie's
preggers. Expect little Savannah or Roy in March.

We have a dry erase board in our kitchen, which hardly
messes with the decor given the room isn't one of metallic Sub-
Zero and granite countertops. New to the board is a clipping from
the *Onion,* a publication that either has diminished in relevance or
is just bound to a demographic to which I no longer belong; it has

been ages since the paper graced our apartment. Tim brought it home recently for one small headline: "Kitten Thinks of Nothing But Murder All Day." Next to this clipping are two wedding invitations: Kim & Shannon, Kevin & Carrie. There is also a handwritten note reminding us to buy coarse ground pepper, though we did this weeks ago.

Kim and Shannon are friends we see regularly. I have not seen Kevin and Carrie for ages, and my last attempt to rectify this fact, a simple happy hour after work, faltered. I had not known at the time of planning the evening that soon afterward I would graze my way onto a website for animal rescue and decide kittens were imperative, the light source in my personal photosynthesis. So we were on our fifth day with the kittens and it was difficult enough for me to leave them home alone during the workday, much less for an extended period afterward. They had demonstrated an insatiable hunger for electrical wires and though we'd taped yards and yards down to the floor, there were some that resisted proofing, namely those tangled behind our television, a tangle the kittens liked to call home sweet home.

In my cancellation email, I stooped to the low of attaching a picture of the kittens, trusting that their adorability would absolve me. Their adorability, I tell you, could inspire the spontaneous generation of tissue, muscle, and valves, hearts bursting in those people who exist with dead spaces in their chests.

Of the guest list, it was Kevin who I most wanted to see—
who has not a dead space in his chest but a full and generous
heart—but the appended picture failed to even trigger a faster
beat. Instead, he expressed not only outright disappointment,
but also a blanket loathing for all cats. I can recall him staying
the night at our apartment long ago, part of a ragtag crew that
obnoxiously barhopped until early morning, and first up the next
day he stepped firmly into a steamy pile of cat shit. He left his
sock in our garbage and went home, grinning, with one foot bare
in his shoe. I cannot recall him denouncing the species. Our cat,
Phoebe Bean, had chronic gastrointestinal problems and, to use
veterinary parlance, rarely eliminated within the litter box. She
preferred the very middle of our foyer. Last year, she suddenly
began wasting away and at four pounds we put her down to a
final sleep. The night before, she lay limp against the sideboards
of our apartment; when she moved, her back legs wobbled and
then collapsed beneath her; she refused food; she took only spots
of water from a spoon. I stayed beside her on the floor, dragging
a blanket and a pillow wherever she drifted, resting soft corners
beneath her head, the edges beneath my body. For short intervals,
she let me hold her close in the cradle of my arm and gently
stroke the cheek beneath her whiskers.

Tim kept watch, took shifts, held us both. He had to go to

work in the morning before our appointment with the vet and for those hours alone with her my repeated wish was that she not die in my arms. I had to keep my arms, they were required features, and if she died in them, my thinking was that, short of amputation, my arms would have to go sleeved for the rest of my days. She spared my arms; she was a good girl. She died as scheduled, under the administrations of our vet, a woman who had put countless animals down and yet still seemed shocked that this one, this cat, was mortal like the rest.

Atop her medical chart was the notation VVVVVVVVVVVC, translating into nothing technical but rather very, very, very, very, very, very, very, very, very, very, very violent cat; for the more delicate portions of her exams, the vet used to fit herself with a pair of cowhide welding gloves that reached her elbows. Phoebe was averse to strangers, a fear born in her first seven years when she lived with someone else, marginalized in that home by a dog and then finally by a baby. I never had a pet and knew nothing of cats. I took her in out of what could only have been a nesting instinct. I had fallen in love, I was nicely coupled, and no matter that I lived in a third-floor hovel in a college town, I was going to make it home to a cat. I neglected to consult my landlord. Phoebe was with me for three weeks before Tim kindly took her into his house, a spacious house they could never afford to fully heat. His housemates found her disagreeable but nevertheless treated her to canned tuna, to which she became downright addicted. The three of us, in this clumsy way, eventually worked our way to one place, another third-floor hovel, this one in Brooklyn, where the family unit solidified. She was not our pet, but our baby, and we cared little if this exalted label caused eyes to roll. She was our baby. We took half of her ashes to our college campus and tossed them near the radio station, where we first met, and vowed there would be no other cat in our lives. She was the sum total, the only, the one. Vows like this must be made all the time.

I am sitting in the backyard patio of a bar after work. Jean is with me and pulls from her bag three wedding planners that her company has published. The plastic table wobbles beneath them. They are not for me but for my cousin, seven years my junior, engaged to be wed in less than a year, an amount of time that feels to me insufficient to plan even one-sixteenth of this wedding. In my mind, I know my cousin will likely leave these planners unused, but procuring wedding planners and thrusting them upon her somehow makes me feel better about the entire affair.

When the marriage question is put to me, and this happens at an approximate rate of once every quarter hour, I don't have the heart to tell people that I would buckle under the planning, that while I can certainly make the essential decision, I am without the constitution to design a wedding, to cull bridal magazines and browse heavy binders, to determine in advance one grand and glorious day. I fear I would come up against invitations and concuss to a blow of paper stock.

To this, people—and by people I mean strangers who have heard of my unmarried status and rushed to find my poor soul on the street—will impart the distinction between wedding and marriage, insinuating, I suppose, a simple town hall union with a witness on break from lunch. I am not sure what town hall looks like and all that I can conjure up is the last madhouse of jury duty assigned to me, and amidst this backdrop, we are being pronounced husband and wife over the waiting room intercom, in between a long recital of juror names, after which we are then scuttled to a selection room and asked if we have relatives in law enforcement; if we have experience dealing with the local police; if we have family or friends practicing law; and to these questions, we both repeat, I do, I do, I do. Town hall, you see, will not do.

There is middle ground, presumably, between a white-drenched, banquet-bursting wedding and one conducted after you run your personal effects through a security scanner, but the problem with middle ground is that its borders are porous:

no chain-link fence, no barbed wire, no wayfarer station, no sign that states Now Leaving Middle Ground. You wander, unaware that you have entered a land of extremes and where you were just throwing together fruit and vegetables and crackers for a picnic spread, you somehow find yourself pureeing large chunks of cantaloupe in the food processor, sweetening the mix with honey, seasoning with minced mint, scrounging for the good thermos in the cabinet of underused kitchenware, going to trouble that is definition opposite of leisurely picnic. At this point, a sign would be of use. Because it won't be until you sit down on the blanket, taking in the clear sky and slight breeze, that you discover the cantaloupe soup is still in the refrigerator and nowhere near the cooler anchoring a corner of the blanket, and only then do you realize that the earth upon which you sit is not middle ground at all. A similar experience occurs when you awaken to a downpour predicted to last the entirety of the day and decide it is perfect weather to see that exhibition at the Guggenheim, only to deplete open museum hours sitting on the couch, thinking about going to the museum while weakly investing in the fates of aspiring designers featured on a marathon of *Project Runway,* which you rationalize could be an art form in the realm of reality television, if compared to, say, *Celebrity Fit Club.* In this case, barbed wire would apply nicely. Point being, for me to remain on middle ground for a prolonged period of time, there'd better be a citadel at its center, fortified and guarded, and at the center of that, a room that locks from the outside. It would be a prison of my own good. I would gaze upon the mortar bricks, and think myself a princess who might let her hair down if it didn't get so frizzy in the moat air. And once you think yourself a princess, well, you are downright primed to plan a wedding.

I thank Jean for the planners. We commiserate a little about the domestication furor that has come over our friends, and how it often becomes all they talk about, leaving us to talk about how it is all they talk about. We discuss how there are many benefits to technology but receiving sonograms via email is not of this number. Carrie sent one in such fashion. As reply, I sent a card, one with an oven sketched on the front, the word "bun" written inside the oven.

Dear Carrie,

I intended on responding to your email but found myself at a loss for sonogram-appropriate things to say (Cute! Adorable! Grainy & Amorphous!). So I did as my mother taught me—when in doubt, buy a cute card. Wishing the months ahead will be healthy and comfortable for you. Love to Chad and the dogs.

Keep me posted but also, and this is important, keep in mind that pregnancy news is best served with a side of nonpregnancy news. :) Happy Gestation!

My grandmother used to bandy about the Italian phrase *testa dura* when one of her precious dears was behaving out of character. It literally translates into "hard head" but means "stubborn." I suppose I have taken *testa dura* and made it a philosophy. I am aware that it will not kill, maim, or even pinch me to indulge in discussions about what songs should serenade the dance between the groom and his mother, or delight with small hand claps in an anecdote about the first plop of poop in the toilet. Yet, my stance is widely known, and it comes as a shock to people when I show signs of unforced interest in grooms or poop. If I dare take a baby into my arms and coo something cutesy, my companions slow their movements to a halt, bracing themselves for the screeching halt of earthly orbit. Reactions like this almost pressure me to live up to my curmudgeonly reputation, otherwise leaving scores of disappointed acquaintances, who were, by the way, just about to change the subject. Out of courtesy. Lest I bristle. Lest I implode.

I suppose I understand the instinct. I take care to talk about the kittens at a length that does not invite the description *ad nauseam.* In fact, I take care not to talk about anything ad nauseam.

I have noticed that I am one of a substantial population who measures and weighs a conversation, who abruptly severs a line of thought by saying, "But enough about that."

A theory would have the attention span so shortened by media habits that we cannot hold focus on one topic for an extended period of time, and those who test that focus automatically qualify as bores. Another theory would blame current foreign policy, forcing us into apologist mode from top to bottom: We are not an affront to your people, your culture, your beliefs, we are sorry to even bring up the existence of our newborn, much less how he howled like the dickens while sitting for his first haircut.

But because the general population has not elected me to speak on its behalf, I can only say that personally it is a reluctance to be defined by any one occupation, enthusiasm, or sentiment. I do not, for instance, want to be taken as the crazy lady with cats, model recipient for mugs, magnets, and cross-stitched pillows that say CURLING UP WITH YOU IS PURR-FECT. I fear being boxed up and labeled in thick permanent marker. Wife. Mother. Cat Fancier. And until I am comfortable putting out into the world whatever pleases me, be it play-by-plays of kitten wrestling or the spawn of my womb, without caution, without check, with no heed to what other people think, then civilization, whose continuance my mother swears rests upon my wedded bliss, will just have to wait.

About the kittens. We sought out kittens on impulse. Though I had modified my stance to thinking that one day in the distant future there would be room in my heart for another cat, I was still in armband mourning for Phoebe Bean. But while there is nothing you can do for a cat who has already died, there is something you can do for cats not yet dead but close, days away from being destroyed for lack of homes. A stray had been meeting me every morning on the way to work, with a hiss, and the venom surged direct to my bloodstream. When it failed to meet me for a full week, I wondered after its fate, and immediately went off in search of its homeless brethren.

Online, I found countless sites of organizations that facilitated rescue and adoption, all posting thumbnail photographs of the animals they had at hand, and the number of these animals totaled something staggering. Any person with brains enough to follow *The Price Is Right* to the very end knows to spay and neuter pets, and while Bob Barker is not my go-to voice of reason for all that life involves, he certainly is in this regard. I kept clicking back to one kitten in particular. She was given the name Mystic, hardly to my fancy, but more inspired than the kittens listed beneath her named Two, Three, and Four.

In an instant message, I downsized the font so small as to suggest a whisper and wrote: *Look what I found.* There was something furtive about the line, as if I actually wrote *Look what I just did.* I was worried that Tim would think this premature. I was more worried that he would think it a betrayal. His thoughts, instead, revolved around cute and its many powers of persuasion. We spent a good portion of the workday messaging each other about the prospect of a kitten, this kitten, and then, to justify earning our salaries for the day, postponed all discussion for a summit to be held after work that night. We met for drinks at a bar near home. The Mets were playing the Braves, and winning; this was early in the season, when it was best to refrain from buying a Reyes T-shirt, otherwise jinxing him to a slump at the plate and the team to its former doom. Going over the finer details, namely if we were ready for a new cat in our lives, our decision seemed obvious from the long list of names we thought better than Mystic, but no decision was verbalized.

The next morning, a Saturday, we went through the motions of breakfast, grocery shopping, and other errands, without speaking of the subject. We were both still turning it over in our heads. Not until late in the day did I say, meekly, "So, we're not going to get her, then?" to which Tim said, "Let's go get her right now." Tim, of course, is the one who bought me the Reyes T-shirt. We called the number and inquired within. Sean Casey, who might as well wear a cape and try his hand at scaling skyscrapers, runs an animal rescue out of his own apartment, specializing in exotics and reptilians, but also housing your basic puppy and kitten. He routinely goes to the city shelter and of the hundreds of animals there brings to his home as many as he can physically handle. Sean Casey told us that Mystic was at the vet with a respiratory infection. In fending off our assurances that we could wait, he insinuated that she might not return. With the detachment that comes with taking in and sending off animals as a matter of course, Sean Casey was having none of our myopia about one kitten. He had two full boxes of kittens and they needed homes. He had some off-site heroics scheduled for the afternoon but could have us over later that night, and at a brisk pace gave us the time and place. Fate had him within walking distance of our apartment. We went to see the boxes.

It is Monday. Around nine. For the past three hours, I have been searching for a cocktail dress to wear to Kevin and Carrie's wedding. In my closet, there are already two dresses hanging in a garment bag with the tags still attached but neither of them proved to be the kind of dress that I wanted to try on and prance around in to see how it moved, to admire its silhouette. To broaden the pool of choices, I decided to just throw cash at the problem, dispensing with department stores and heading direct to boutiques: Scoop, Kirna Zabête, BCBG, Anna Sui, Marc Jacobs, Seize sur Vingt, D&G, Prada, Bottega Veneta, Vivienne Tam, Catherine Malandrino, Klee, Bird, Neda, Goldy and Mac, Eidolon, Flirt, Lucia, La Vedette. There may be others. Did I mention this was a dress for a wedding not my own?

I found a dress at Bird, a boutique in Brooklyn, that I really liked, at a price I liked not so much. When it comes to throwing cash at the problem, my windup is slow and exaggerated, and balks ensue. I paced outside the shop until it closed, purchasing only further hours with which to fret over this dress. Now I am throwing together a meal of assorted vegetables and chicken sausage, hoping there is a dressing in the refrigerator that will glue the tastes together. Hugo is directly between my feet as I stand at the counter chopping vegetables, because something will drop, he knows it, something will drop and he will be there when it does, blind to the cherry tomato that Silas is dribbling down the hall with adroitness that will have him striking for the English Premiership in about a year.

Tim walks through the door and is barely unburdened of his bag when I recount my fruitless search for a dress. He asks about the dresses already bought, unsympathetic to my inability to prance around in them in bare feet while listening to the new

Justin Timberlake single. Hearing of the dress that came close tonight, he tells me to just buy it already, advice that would not be endorsed by Suze Orman or the guy who claims money spent on daily lattes is equal to a down payment on a starter home. Nevertheless, this is all I need to hear; in the morning, I will delay my arrival at work and be at the shop the minute it opens. Despite the fact that there is a minuscule ashy smudge on the left strap and the cut could be a tad less boxy, the dress is more perfect than all of the dresses hanging in the city.

My hands sticky with ponzu sauce, I amend my list. I do not work with a handheld device or a day planner but rather a yellow legal pad: There is a Thursday column, and indented beneath that is a Wedding subset. Sometimes, I wonder how I manage to do anything at all. The majority of functioning human beings do not routinely employ checkboxes for lists that sometimes consist of nothing more than *coffee, office, gum.* My current list feels justifiable, however, and I insert *Bird dress* in the narrow row just below Thursday and right before *office, eyebrows, ATM, umbrella, anniversary card, thing for blister, yoga, start packing.* I add nothing to the Wedding subset, as *dress!!!* is already there.

In the morning, I check online for store hours and find that Bird doesn't open until 11:30 and while I can slip into work as late as 10:30, another hour is just plain delinquent. I am not good at delinquency in the daylight hours. I go into work according to normal schedule and though Tim, with more sage advice, tells me to call the shop and ask them to hold it for me until after work, I fail to do this. My thinking—and calling it thinking is a work of great generosity—is that if this dress is meant to be mine it will be there to greet me. So sure that we will be together, I don't even head straight from work to the shop. I go to buy shoes. I go to buy shoes for a dress that is not yet an official possession. I also slip into a bookstore and browse a bit. I take my fucking time. I swing my bags of shoes and books and swerve into Brooklyn on the subway with the excitement that comes with finally being done with something. On my list, this will be a magnificent box to check. In fact, two magnificent boxes.

When I walk in the shop I already know the dress is gone. Two were hanging on the farthest rack in the back, light in color between grays and blacks. The swath of taupe is slender now, signaling the choices have thinned to just one, and because the dress was cut a bit boxy, surely someone who would have ordinarily gone with the medium has bought the small.

I approach the dress slowly and pry the label into the light. I take the dress to the counter and ask the girl if there are any more, in that back room that all stores have and produce such miracles that retailers ought to cultivate ideas for world peace amongst racks of surplus. The clerk knows there are no others in the store but their other location, a few neighborhoods over, may have more. A few clicks on a spreadsheet and she confirms what even the mannequins could have told me.

Outside on the pavement, I shed tears over this dress, even as that ashy smudge still bothers me, even as the boxy cut still bothers me, even as my disproportionate reaction bothers me, because what I'd like to do at this moment is call a girlfriend and cry over this dress until it feels rightly silly and meet for a drink and talk anything but dresses but all my girlfriends are at a distance, geographically or otherwise.

At home, the kittens are at the door, in wait. They headbutt my ankles and seem perplexed that these moves fail to drop me horizontally. Silas takes to biting any part of my leg below the knee while Hugo jumps to the nick in the hallway wall that he may believe is a nuclear button. I bend down and they come to chew the ends of my hair.

I sit with them as they eat from refreshed bowls, and they take pauses to look at me, making sure there is no move to make another one of those inexplicable departures that plague their lives. They have discussed this matter and concluded that it would be best for everyone involved if we all kept to the apartment with no leave whatsoever. Still pending is their decision on whether to let us sleep uninterrupted through the night; at an impasse, the subject will be taken up after they render extinct the shoelace species.

It is my first experience with kittens, and my first experience with male cats. With Tim, with Hugo, with Silas, the home is one of boys. When Sean Casey brought out the boxes, I gravitated first to a girl, only four weeks old, the only girl of both litters he had to show, and we were that close to taking her home, except that it seemed only right for her to have a companion. The hours we spent away from the apartment, between work and errands and commutes and park runs and bike rides and dinners and drinks and shows and films and holidays—those hours never sat well with me, knowing that Phoebe Bean grew lonely; for as characteristically aloof and independent as she was, she missed us dearly, and would stay petulantly angry for a bit before pressing herself to our legs, our laps, our arms.

Bringing just one home was not within my capacity. In search of a second, one worked us over fast with his eyes, blue with violet flashes, but this one, this boy of eight weeks, already had a companion, a scrawny gray thing that seemed attached to his hindquarters. Tim lifted the gray thing to eye level and gave him the once-over. Sean Casey had precious time and a crowd had formed around the boxes, a few serious takers in the bunch. There

Michele Mortimer

was no time to think, to nurture a decision; there was no time to wait for a sign, a shift in winds or the reach of a paw. The boys were in hand. And so they were ours. We left the little girl behind.

Kevin and Carrie are married in a castle. Seriously. There is a castle on the campus of Manhattanville College in Purchase, New York, about an hour north of the city, and it is a castle of warmth, with hardwood floors and oriental rugs, stained glass, and windowed doors that allow ample fresh air and a view of three or four indescribable greens. There is no moat but the day is humid; my hair repudiates the hot iron treatment and frizzes, then flips, up and out at the ends, surely making guests wonder if it was really necessary to put the bop in the bop shoo bop shoo bop.

The ceremony, held in the main drawing room, is neither religious nor traditional, but rather a casual exchange of vows, words the bride and groom wrote themselves, and facilitated by a generic officiant who makes parenthetical jokes just as light and sweet. Just before the pronouncement of husband and wife, we are asked to take a moment to ponder the notion of love: to think of those we love, and why we love them. I rest my hand on Tim's knee. A casual observer would think that I am taking this moment to think of him, of our love over the years, of our connection deep and profound, and possibly question why this left hand of mine, so firmly placed on his knee, is without a ring, but a casual observer would not see past the flipped ends of my hair, where my face is clenched so not to emit a giggle. I am actually using his knee to brace myself. I cannot help but think this moment of silent reflection a silly feature of an otherwise heartfelt ceremony, one that was doing nicely to keep with the gravitational force and remain bound to earth.

Looking at my program for the fifteenth time, I realize that I was thinking about love through the opening remarks, the promises of commitment and companionship, the slipping of rings, and two mumbled readings. Not until it became a *requirement* of the guests to think about love did my thoughts wander to canapés and champagne. We are at a wedding, last I checked. Odds are that our minds will alight on love. Must we *be told?* Perchance I am not married because it feels much like a requirement, and without religion to stiffen this requirement, without baby pangs to soften it, without the disposable income to dress it up in a wedding, for the time being my stance will be contrarian. Having been with someone for ten years, ten years mutually considered the first ten, we feel married according to us, a nonchalance that is healthy for two people so orderly our magazine piles are never askew.

Our table at the reception is number thirteen. The eight of us take collective delight in this cursed assignment. Tim and I are seated with two couples and two bachelors, all dear friends of mine. Drunk before even the salad course, we begin singing at the top of our lungs "Oh Sherrie," which, oddly, disturbs none of our neighbors. *Oh Sherrie! Our love! Holds on! Holds on!* The video for this song—should each panel of the storyboard not be impressed upon your memory—begins with a brief scene in which Steve Perry, lead singer and master of the feathered mullet, is frocked in medieval crown and nobility robe, waiting for his princess bride to walk down the aisle. She walks very, very slowly, because while her head is the size of a head, her veil could serve as a slipcover to a showroom sedan; she actually has to *hoist* it upward to reveal her face. Attendants gather around the couple. Two horn players gaze from a balcony above. Steve Perry reaches his hands toward the bride and then hesitates, shifting his eyes from side to side to take stock of what he is about to do. "This is ridiculous!" he cries out. A wide zoom betrays that we are not in an indeterminate era between medieval and Renaissance times but actually on a contemporary soundstage. A clapboard signals Take Six. These industry sorts seem to know little of Steve Perry, thinking him able to bring verisimilitude to this role of valiant prince when what he brings is star power and a smooth croon to eighties rock. He shakes himself out of the scene, this time for good, stripping away his regal garment. The director (identifying prop: megaphone) pleads his case: "But what about the kidnapping of the princess?! . . . What about the battle to death between good and evil?!" Steve Perry, now in snug jeans and a shirt unbuttoned to reveal the finery of his chest hair, tries to explain: "This is a love song! It has nothing to do with . . . with *this!*" This, meaning the faux castle set and courtly narrative. He darts through extras and stagehands and breaks away from a blowsy manager snapping about interviews and budgets (identifying prop: designer sunglasses). Finally— finally!—Steve Perry finds respite in an empty corridor. He sits himself down on the steps, rests his head back against the cold, hard wall, and sings his love song *the way he wants to sing it, damn it,* to the girl he really loves, with passionate pumps of his fist, with only a broom to use for the overwrought guitar parts. In the end, this cute blond girl, in a plain white tank dress, playfully shoves a fedora atop his head, and they walk off into the back lot together, happily ever after.

The girl in the video was actually his girlfriend, and her name was, in fact, Sherrie. Sadly, they broke up, but the song still works its magic because I am in love with my table. I dote on my boyfriend, I flirt with my bachelor friends, I plot excursions for us couples, like bowling and antiquing. I am in love with

Table Thirteen. We are categorically a fun table, toeing the line of obnoxious here and there, but my sense—and I'm lucky that one of the five still functions—is that there is enough revelry about for us to blend in without incident. It feels safe here, with them, to be a little juvenile, a little silly. My mother made me wait until I was twelve to get my ears pierced; fourteen to wear any black article of clothing; sixteen to wear makeup; seventeen to drive; eighteen to get an after-school job. Her mission as a parent was to keep me from growing up too fast. She did a superlative job. I have hit thirty and am pacing myself to the rites of passage that will have me sacrifice things that still mean something to me, even if they look crude and splashy next to a dignified sonogram.

I think of Carrie a few times, and vow to return her call soon; it is long overdue and with a wedding under my belt, tradition will have me ready for pregnancy. I think this, before thinking only one thought repeatedly and that is to catapult my four-inch heels to the nearest ditch where they can never do harm to my feet again. They are black patent leather and set off the matte black bodice of my dress nicely; from an empire waist, printed georgette silk flows down to just below the knee, taupe and crème giving way to a hem of sunset red; spaghetti straps crisscross in the back. It is a dress I love wearing, as it turns out, though the flow of it, the give of it, has a maternity feel, as if a bump is being concealed.

Wheeled to our hotel room on a luggage cart, I bunch the silk up high between my spread legs and hold a bottle of champagne triumphantly in the air. On the remote chance anyone thinks I am pregnant, this hussy pose should clear things up posthaste.

We are back within city limits. It is not yet noon. We stop in Queens and drop off Kim and Shannon, who in three weeks will be hosting their own wedding, at which we will do this all over again. They wearily pry their bags from the trunk; we wearily say goodbye. In a few days, the four of us will meet for our standing happy hour, a ritual we established to stave off the complacency that had set in over time. Until then, a friend is in town from London and we'll be seeing him for a show, and whatever else we can fit in before he leaves. We will sleep, maybe, next weekend.

Our drive home is quiet. I puzzle together random recollections of the night before. Tim colors in the details. I add to my list: *Call Carrie*. Tim fiddles with the radio, looking for music that will soothe the hangover. At the apartment, a quick scan finds no apparent damage, just toys scattered about. The kittens greet us, Hugo with a whine that he cuts up into short notes, while Silas squeaks almost beneath audible range. Both run directly underfoot.

On the dry erase board is a note from Sung, a friend of ours who lives in the building. We watch his cats, Cleo and Sea Bass, and he returns the favor with Hugo and Silas. The note says: *These cats eat flesh.* While this is Sung's sense of humor at work, it rings close enough to true for us to cringe before laughing. The boys run to the bed and flop to their sides, but to serious petting, they give back teeth, sharp little things that sometimes draw blood. Our kittens would gladly eat flesh. They are young, they are excited, they are animals. Not everyone, after all, domesticates without a fight.

On a Scale of
One to Ten . . .

Megan McMorris

The story is not unique. Those following along at home
will recognize the plotline: Boy meets girl. Boy falls for
girl. Boy and girl decide to buy a house. Boy takes a hard look at
girl's cat. Boy wonders aloud if cat is part of the package.

"So, how old is your cat, anyway?" my boyfriend, Eric, asks
casually one day before we move in.

"Six!" I respond enthusiastically, looking down lovingly at
Lily's chubby tabby cheeks and lime green eyes.

"And, um, how long do these things live again?"

"Oh, cats live long lives. Even, like, *twenty years* sometimes!"

His eyebrows furrow.

"Don't worry. You guys are going to be two peas in a pod
before long, I know it," I assure him.

And there begins my quest to bring these two together. (Eric, look how cute it is when Lily flips over to show us her tummy! Lily, look how comfy Eric's lap is and how expertly he scratches your ears! And how nice is it when he plays hunt-the-laser-dot with you?)

How did it all turn out? You be the judge. What follows is the highlight reel of their first six months together.

April 2006: Month One

I come home on the second day after we've moved in, and yell out a greeting.

He doesn't respond. Even though his truck is outside and I know he's home.

I find him on the floor hooking up his big-screen TV to his DVD player and stereo (which, since he has one of the biggest TVs I've ever seen, is a complicated process, it turns out).

He fixes me with a glare.

"Your cat peed on all my clothes!"

I go upstairs to confirm that, indeed, all of the bags that hold our clothes—which we haven't had a chance to unpack—have recently been used as Lily's litter box.

In her defense, I know that these things happen when a cat is moving. She's trying to establish her territory, she doesn't like change and she's acting out, and besides, she tends to go for dirty clothes on the floor when she needs to relieve her kitty bladder.

Eric sees it a different way. To him, it's just a small animal using his clothes as a toilet. Not that I can blame him (and make no mistake, it's not that I exactly love this habit of hers!), but let's just say there are certain things one gets used to, *puts up with* even, with one's own animal.

I get to test the endurance of our shiny new washer and dryer the next day, and I research how to make cats stop peeing (use a citrus scent and, well, don't leave clothes on the floor). We agree to keep our closet doors closed at all times, because she also takes a liking to shoes when she's choosing a prime spraying spot. Problem solved.

Problem solved to *me*, anyway. To Eric, this day goes down in history as the Day a Cat Peed on My Clothes, and that's when he starts what I've now dubbed the point system. "You know, on a scale of one to ten, your cat is a negative twenty right now!" (Of course, it's always "your cat" when he's mad at her; he calls her by her name on good days.)

Now, if you think about it, this score just isn't fair. "Cut a cat a break—she should at least start out with a zero, don't you think?" my mom chimes in when I tell her about Lily's rating. I *do* think. Still, I'm not too worried. Lily, too, will rise above this like a professional. *Soon, he will be smitten with the kitten,* I say to myself, rubbing my hands together maniacally.

We have our work cut out for us.

Lily's score: negative twenty.

Lily

April 2006: Month One

Two weeks after we move in, we go on a weekend getaway to Ashland, a small town in southern Oregon. We're only gone for three days, so we (read: I) just leave some food and water for Lily. In the back of my mind, I'm a little worried about what she might get up to—after all, she's just getting used to a new house and then we go and abandon her; who knows how she'll show her disgust!—but I keep my worries to myself.

When we open our front door, all we hear is loud meowing from upstairs. I run up and there she is, stuck in the spare bedroom (the door has closed in the wind and we haven't thought to prop the doors open with anything, a lesson duly noted for future trips away). She's used the room as her litter box, but a funny thing happens: Eric isn't mad at her.

"Poor thing, you were locked in there and had to go to the bathroom, didn't you?" he says, scratching her chin.

Lily wanders around for over an hour that night, meowing constantly to tell us her sob story. We laugh about how she seems to calm down for a minute, only to start up again with her meowing, as if she's decided she has more to tell us after all: "And furthermore . . . " "And *then* guess what happened . . . "

Lily's score: two (sympathy points, but I'll take what I can get).

May 2006: Month Two

Despite our best efforts to keep our closet doors closed and to not leave clothes on the floor, we realize there's one more area that we need to tend to: bathmats. For some reason, she sees one and instantly uses it as a ladies' room.

"Goddamn it! Your goddamned cat!" I hear him yelling from his bathroom upstairs. "Where is she?"

As much as I try and explain that you can't teach cats not to do something unless you catch them in the act (or at least so I've heard; I haven't actually tried it), he's not buying it. "You're telling me that a cat has room in her brain to decide to pee on my bathmat but not to know the word 'no'?"

Well, *yes.*

He tries anyway. I'm in the next room when I hear some clatter and crashing, a small meow, and him yelling, "No! *No!*" I come into the room to find him with Lily in his arms, pushing her nose into the bathmat to show her that this is most definitely *not,* he repeats, *not,* a litter box.

She looks up at me with a bored expression.

`Lily's score: negative twenty.`

May 2006: Month Two

I'm in New York City for a book tour, in midtown Manhattan during rush hour traffic, when I see that I have a cell phone message.

It's Eric.

"Give me a call; someone woke me up at four in the morning last night." I'm kind of annoyed—I mean, what does he want me to do about it when I'm across the country from them?

I call back. "So, what happened?" I ask, bracing myself for the words, "Your damn cat! You know what she did?"

Amid the honking horns of NYC cabbies and the squeaking wheels of the city buses, I can barely make out what he's saying, but it seems to me that this story is not what I was expecting to hear (or maybe I'm not hearing him correctly?).

Turns out, he has left the bedroom window open overnight (it *is* May, after all), but it's an uncharacteristically cold night. He wakes up at 4:00 AM to a combination of hard-to-place sensations: a vibration, light tapping, and a heating pad warmth on his left side.

He looks over to find Lily curled into his armpit, purring loudly and kneading away at his shoulder. "I would normally have been mad that she woke me up, but it was so cute I couldn't move her," he tells me. "I think she'd been cold because of the open window, and she looked so happy that she was warm!"

I beam.

Lily's score: seven.

June 2006: Month Three

My sister Erin and I are on a weekend spa getaway with our mom when my sister asks how Lily is doing, pointwise (she's heard about the system and has taken a keen interest in her furry niece's fate). I relay the story about when I was in NYC, which she finds hysterical. "It's always when you're gone that those two get along best, because they're forced to bond," she says.

I agree. I envision the two of them sitting together on the couch watching TV as we speak. "I'm sure she'll be up to about a nine by the time I get back!" I say confidently.

Of course, I've since realized that when it comes to matters of Man and His Girlfriend's Cat, there is no rhyme or reason.

The first tip-off that something is amiss: Lily is especially cuddly with me when I get home, and if you know cats (which I assume you do, if you're reading this), you know this isn't the norm after they've been abandoned for a few days. Typically, Lily ignores me and goes straight to Eric when I return from a trip, even going so far as to climb across my lap to get to his.

It turns out that while I was gone, Eric has gotten acquainted with another cat trait: romping during the middle of the night. Normally this doesn't bother us because we sleep upstairs (Lily prefers to conduct her prowling downstairs), but we're having a heat wave, so he's been sleeping on the living room couch next to the air conditioner. All night, Lily has meowed and raced down the length of the house, and then as a grand finale to the madness decided to take a little bathroom break on the jeans he's left on the floor.

I try to run damage control, reminding him of all the cute things that Lily does—remember that upside-down look she does? Or when she kneads? You *love* that!—but he isn't amused.

Lily's score: negative fifty.

July 2006: Month Four

I decide to give the cat a chat. "Okay, kiddo, listen up." I put my arm around her little furry shoulder one day when he's gone. "I'm only going to say this once, so pay attention. This guy, he doesn't just become smitten at the drop of a hat. You've got to work it. Don't just walk the catwalk, *own* it, girl. That way you turn your head over and look at him upside down, displaying your tummy? He loves it. So do it. Often. When you're sleeping? Go ahead and put that paw right over your eyes—it kills him every time. The kneading? He thinks it's hilarious. So knead, Lily, *knead like you've never kneaded before!* And throw in some loud purring while you're at it!"

Exhausted by my pep talk, I sit down on the couch. Lily blinks at me and stalks off. You see, she doesn't do that "man-pleasing" thing. In fact, it's what my sister likes most about her. One time, after cat-sitting for me, she offers up her assessment of my little beast. "The thing about Lily? She's her own cat. I admire that in a cat. She doesn't care what people think, and she's not shy." It's true: Lily, blissfully ignorant of where she stands on the point system, doesn't care. As far as she's concerned, she's fine just the way she is.

Lily's score: still negative fifty (if you take the optimist's approach, you could say that she has nowhere to go but up).

August 2006: Month Five

I come home from my book club meeting to find Eric watching TV, Lily right next to him. "Oh, look at you guys—just two peas in a pod," is my favorite thing to say upon seeing this.

I plop down on the couch.

"Lily moved up in points while you were gone," Eric says without taking his eyes off the TV screen.

The magical number-raising technique: At one point in the night, he looks over to see Lily curled up, sleeping, with her paw covering her eyes.

Atta girl.

`Lily's score: five.`

September 2006: Month Six

So, will this story have a happy ending? The jury is still out. If it will please that jury, though, I would like to present a few pieces of evidence that will show—without a reasonable doubt—that this is a guy who has warmed up considerably to Life with a Cat.

1. A couple weeks ago, I come outside to the back yard to find him laughing at Lily, who is investigating the newly mown grass. We sit and laugh as she carefully makes her way across the yard and then freezes when she sees her shadow against the fence in the early-evening light, thinking it's another cat. As Eric starts laughing, her ears go back toward us, and that makes him laugh harder because her ears in the shadow move, too. "You know," he says, "I have to admit there are subtle things about cats that are funny, but you just have to live with them for a while before you notice them." Can I have a witness?

2. Last week, Eric stretches out on the couch by the fireplace, reading a magazine, and Lily curls up next to him, half of her body on a pillow and half on his leg. Every time she assumes a comfier position (you know that cat progression: one paw curled, then extended, then a heavy sigh, then a kitty dream complete with whole-body twitches), Eric calls out softly to me and tells me to look at her. After each time, he starts reading his magazine again, putting it up in front of his face. Slight prob, though: He doesn't realize that the way he's holding the magazine still shows his right cheek. Which is bunched up into a grin.

3. Two days ago, Lily is throwing up. I'm out late gabbing away with my friend Abby when he calls, and he's clearly not happy that he's spent time cleaning up the carpet (not that I can blame him). He says he's going to put her in the laundry room (where her food and water are) because he's going to sleep. When I come home and open the laundry room door, I expect to see her meowing pathetically on the cold floor. Instead, she's lazing on a pillow, one of three that Eric has put in there for her. He has even gone so far as to open the washing machine and put a pillow inside, so she'll be cozy in there (which is cat heaven!). When I tell him that this is most certainly a sign that the little girl is growing on him, he attempts an alternate version of the story. "I told her

that I was giving her five minutes until I closed the door, so she should get whatever she needs to make herself comfortable, and she dragged those pillows in there herself."

As much as he denies his true feelings about the cat, though, they're hard to cover up. After all, I can still see that cheek bulging up into a smile when he thinks I'm not looking.

Lily's current score range: negative one when she relieves her kitty bladder in an inappropriate spot (a far cry from the totally unfair negative fifty) to seven on a good day.

Acknowledgments

The coolest part of putting together an anthology is that you don't have to do it alone. Twenty-eight other women worked on the words on these pages, and I learned something from each of them. Here's a toast to all the contributors who willingly devoted their time and energies to this collection. Special thanks to writers I personally begged to take part: Dimity McDowell, Lisa L. Goldstein, Heather Gowen Walsh, Jenna Schnuer, Susan Schulz Wuornos, Barrie Gillies, Tracy Teare, Amy Fishbein Brightfield, Judy Sutton Taylor, Kristen Kemp, and Clea Simon. And thanks to those I "met" through the dog-book process and who lived to tell another tale: Melinda J. Combs, Margaret Littman, Sarah Shey, Kathryn Renner, and Susan T. Lennon.

To my editor at Seal Press, Jill Rothenberg, a big hug for

having this whole women/animal anthology idea in the first place (whatever will you brainstorm next?), and for providing two wise eyeballs for each essay—your edits and suggestions made everything that much better. It's a rare and lucky thing to have such a fantastic collaboration with an editor and to feel so encouraged every step of the way.

Thanks to my seasoned cat-sitting sister Erin, for entertaining me with pictures from your cat-caretaker gigs across the country, and for always lending an ear about Lily's latest tribulations.

Thanks also to Eric, for your patience with said cat and in putting up with the many ups and downs that come with sharing your space with the little rugrat.

And, of course, a little ear scratch and a warm lap for Lily, for keeping me company by snoring next to me as I worked on this book.

About the
Contributors

Amy Fishbein Brightfield is the senior health
editor at *Fitness* magazine. She's worked as an editor at
Woman's Day and *Seventeen*, and she has been published in *New
York* magazine's special weddings issue and on iVillage.com. She's
the author of *The Truth about Girlfriends,* a book about friendship
for teenage girls. Miss Kitty is still living large in her NYC pad.

Melinda J. Combs's fiction and nonfiction have appeared in *Woman's
Best Friend: Women Writers on the Dogs in Their Lives, Far from Home:
Father-Daughter Travel Adventures, Urban Dog, Salome, .ISM Quarterly,
Clean Sheets, Orange Coast,* and other journals. She also teaches at
a variety of schools, including Orange County High School of the
Arts. When she's not being entertained by her students, she writes
and travels. She lives in Huntington Beach, California.

Dallas-based freelance writer Sophia Dembling's articles and essays have appeared in the *Dallas Morning News* (where her essay for this book originally appeared), the *Chicago Tribune, Salon,* and *Beliefnet,* among other newspapers, magazines, and websites. She's also the author of *The Yankee Chick's Survival Guide to Texas.* She's been catless for five years now (and must admit that she's enjoying life without a litter box), but she has recently become acquainted with the pleasures of dog ownership.

Sue Dickman is a freelance writer in Easthampton, Massachusetts. Her essays and articles have appeared in the *Christian Science Monitor,* the *San Francisco Chronicle, Amherst* magazine, and the *Readerville Journal,* and her short stories have been published in *Puerto del Sol* and *Passages North.*

Carol Driscoll is a Boulder, Colorado–based freelance writer. Her essays and articles have been published in the *Christian Science Monitor, Fine Gardening, Dayspa, St. Louis Post-Dispatch,* and *Canadian Homes and Cottages,* among others.

Barrie Gillies is a senior editor at *Parents* magazine in New York City. No matter how hard she tries, she hasn't gotten Will—

or Annie, for that matter—on the cover. Will can say "dog" (okay, "du") but not "cat" or "Annie." Go figure.

Lisa L. Goldstein was the editor in chief of *Fit* and the executive editor of *Living Fit*. She's been a freelance writer and editor for *Men's Health, Harper's Bazaar, Self,* and many other magazines. Her favorite things in life include baking homemade bread, reading, running, watching baseball, having a false sense of well-being, twirling her hair around her finger, and rubbing her cats' bellies. She lives just outside of New York City.

Lisa Guernsey is the copy chief at *Domino* magazine. Lisa has worked at *Working Woman, Harper's Bazaar, Martha Stewart Living, Parents,* and *Ticker* magazines, and an article of hers has been published in *Hog River Journal,* a Connecticut historical quarterly. She lives in Brooklyn, New York.

Linda Kay Hardie is a freelance writer and editor, and is the author of *Louie Larkey and the Bad Dream Patrol* (Moon Mountain, 2001). Her articles have appeared in magazines such as *Cat Fancy* and *Chile Pepper*. She lives in Reno, Nevada, with her three Abyssinian cats.

Jennifer Jalalat received her MFA in creative writing from Chapman University. Her work has been published in *.ISM Quarterly*. She teaches English at the college level and has been roommates with her cat, Dulcinea, for ten happy years. She lives in Huntington Beach, California.

Freelance writer *Kristen Kemp* has written for *Self, Glamour, Ladies' Home Journal, CosmoGIRL!, Girls' Life, Marie Claire,* the *New York Daily News, Men's Health,* and others. Before that, she was an associate editor at *Cosmopolitan,* a staff writer at *Twist,* and an assistant editor at *Girls' Life.* Kristen is the author of twelve young adult books, fiction and nonfiction. Her latest teen novel is *Breakfast at Bloomingdale's* (Scholastic, 2007). She lives in the New York City metro area with several short people and sewing projects.

Valerie Cabrera Krause is the coauthor of *The Bridal Wave: A Survival Guide to the Everyone-I-Know-Is-Getting-Married Years* (Villard, 2007). She lives in Los Angeles with her husband, Tommy, their dog, Stella, and their two cats, Ernest and Phoebe. When she is not watching something inappropriate for her lifestage on TV (*The Hills, Next,* anyone?), reading trashy novels, or growing irate over myriad small annoyances, she may be found riding her bicycle around the streets of Los Angeles.

Susan T. Lennon is a freelance writer whose work has appeared in *Newsweek,* the *Washington Post, USA Weekend, Health, Prevention,* and others. She works from home with Atticus and his Labrador retriever "brother," Harley, whose story appeared in *Woman's Best Friend: Women Writers on the Dogs in Their Lives.* She and her husband live in Rocky Hill, Connecticut. Her website is www.susanlennon.com.

Margaret Littman is a Chicago-based writer whose dogs, Natasha and Cooper, won't allow a cat to step paw in her house. And she likes it like that. Her work has appeared in *Woman's Best Friend: Women Writers and the Dogs in Their Lives,* as well as in *Wine Enthusiast, Woman's Day, Art and Antiques,* and many other publications. She is the author of *The Dog Lover's Companion to Chicago.*

Dimity McDowell lives in Colorado Springs, Colorado, with her cat-allergic husband, two kids, and *(sigh)* a dog. An editor at large for *Shape* magazine, she also writes for *Real Simple* and *Outside,* among others.

Michele Mortimer lives in Brooklyn with her boyfriend and two kittens. She has an MFA from New York University and currently works in publishing. While her forays into fiction have been published in literary journals, this is her first essay in print.

Suz Redfearn is a freelance writer whose work has appeared in the *Washington Post, Slate, Salon,* and *Men's Health,* as well as in many essay collections and on public radio. Redfearn dwells in Falls Church, Virginia, with her husband, Marty, her daughter, Evangeline, her golden retriever, Ike, and the inimitable Habbib, who is somewhere between eleven and fifteen years old. His black markings are graying now and he has problems jumping up on chairs, but he still finds energy to continue his work on the decor.

Kathryn Renner is a freelance writer, essayist, and radio talk show host in Bellevue, Washington. Her work has appeared in the *Christian Science Monitor,* the *Chicago Tribune, Better Homes and Gardens, Reader's Digest, Horizon Air,* and others. Her most recent essay appeared in *Woman's Best Friend: Women Writers on the Dogs in Their Lives.*

Jenna Schnuer is a NYC-based freelance writer. A contributing editor for *American Way,* the American Airlines magazine, and a columnist for *Pages,* she has almost perfected the art of stopping Maynard from biting her ankles while she works. Sort of. Well, not really.

Sarah Shey has written for the *New York Times, Time Out New York,* the *Forward,* the *Philadelphia Inquirer, This Old House,* the *Des Moines Register,* and the *Iowan,* among others. She wrote two children's books set in Iowa, *Sky All Around* and *Blue Lake Days,* and contributed to *Woman's Best Friend: Women Writers on the Dogs in Their Lives.* She is at work on a nonfiction narrative.

Clea Simon is the author of the Theda Krakow mysteries *(Mew Is for Murder* and *Cattery Row)* and several nonfiction books, including *The Feline Mystique: On the Mysterious Connection Between Women and Cats.* She lives in Cambridge, Massachusetts, with her husband, Jon, and their cat, Musetta. Her website is www .cleasimon.com.

Judy Sutton Taylor is convinced that she's microchipped to attract every stray dog and cat within a twenty-mile radius of wherever she happens to be. She's been bringing home pets ever since she was a kid in Brooklyn, and she now lives in Chicago with a small menagerie of dogs and cats, twin toddlers, and one very patient husband. When she's not saving furry creatures, she's the Kids editor at *Time Out Chicago,* and a freelance writer for other magazines and newspapers.

Tracy Teare lives in Falmouth, Maine, with her husband, three daughters, one black Lab, and zero cats. A freelance writer, she specializes in fitness, health, and parenting. Tracy's work has been published in *Health, Cooking Light, Prevention, Fitness, Shape, Family Fun,* and *Body + Soul,* and she is the coauthor of *Pedometer Walking* and *Walking Through Pregnancy and Beyond.*

Erin Torneo has written for *Lucky, Cosmopolitan, Seed,* the *Independent, indieWIRE, Mother Earth News, Variety,* and *Kyoto Journal.* She is coauthor of *The Bridal Wave: A Survival Guide to the Everyone-I-Know-Is-Getting-Married Years.* She lives in Los Angeles and New York with her cat, Sashi, and her fiancé, Sascha.

Lynne Truss is a writer and journalist who started out as a literary editor with a blue pencil and then got sidetracked. The author of three novels and numerous radio comedy dramas, she spent six years as the television critic of the *Times* of London, followed by four (rather peculiar) years as a sports columnist for the same newspaper. She won Columnist of the Year for her work for *Women's Journal.* She is the author of the number-one bestseller *Eats, Shoots and Leaves: Why, Commas Really Do Make a Difference!* which has sold more than one million copies and won the national British Award; *Talk to the Hand: The Utter Bloody Rudeness of the World Today, or Six Good Reasons to Stay Home and Bolt the Door;* and *The Lynne Truss Treasury,* where this essay first appeared. She lives in Brighton, England.

Heather Gowen Walsh is a freelance writer in Darien, Connecticut. She has worked as an editor at *Parents* and *Fitness* magazines. Last she heard, the Sophster was still spreading her eye gunk and kneading her new owner every day.

Susan Schulz Wuornos is the editor in chief of *CosmoGIRL!* magazine in New York City. In addition to writing to her readers monthly in her editor's letter and publishing as many pet and animal-activism articles as possible, her work has also appeared in magazines such as *Redbook, Good Housekeeping,* and *Shape.*

Journalist Leah A. Zeldes's work appears regularly in the *Chicago Sun-Times*, the *Daily Herald*, and other regional and national publications. Her short fiction, which has been described as "ludicrously imaginative," has appeared in a number of anthologies, most notably *Sherlock Holmes in Orbit* and *Women Writing Science Fiction as Men* (both from DAW Books).

About the Editor

Megan Mc Morris is the author of *Oregon Hiking*, coauthor of *Pacific Northwest Hiking*, and editor of *Woman's Best Friend: Women Writers on the Dogs in Their Lives*. Her magazine articles have appeared in *Self, Runner's World, Cooking Light, Woman's Day, Glamour,* and *Fitness,* among others. She lives in Portland, Oregon, where she's currently working on a guidebook to her city; *Moon Portland* will be published in 2008. Her website is www.meganmcmorris.com.

Selected Titles from Seal Press

For more than thirty years, Seal Press has published groundbreaking books. *By women. For women. Visit our website at www.sealpress.com.*

Go Your Own Way edited by Faith Conlon, Ingrid Emerick & Christina Henry de Tessan. $15.95, 1-58005-199-6. An inspiring collection of essays, life experiences, and insights from journeys and adventures of women who travel the world solo, on their own terms.

Woman's Best Friend edited by Megan McMorris. $14.95, 1-58005-163-4. An offbeat and poignant collection about those four-legged friends a girl can't do without.

The Bigger, The Better, the Tighter the Sweater edited by Samantha Schoech and Lisa Taggart. $14.95, 1-58005-210-X. A refreshingly honest and funny collection of essays on how women view their bodies.

Rescue Me, He's Wearing a Moose Hat by Sherry Halperin. $13.95, 1-58005-068-9. The hilarious account of a woman who finds herself back in the dating scene after midlife.

Women Who Win by Lisa Taggart. $14.95, 1-58005-200-2. Bypassing the usual routine of sound bites and training regimes, Taggart delves into what really inspires each professional woman in her individual sport and reveals what makes her tick.

Dirty Sugar Cookies by Ayun Halliday. $14.95, 1-58005-150-2. Ayun Halliday is back with essays about her disastrous track record in the kitchen and her culinary observations.